MW00872661

ERADICATING AMERICAN "PROSECUTOR MISCONDUCT":

A Handbook for Prosecutors,
Criminal Defense Attorneys,
and Others Interested in Criminal Justice

Ronald H. Clark
Distinguished Practitioner in Residence
Seattle University School of Law

ISBN 9798376310014

TABLE OF CONTENTS

This book and I am dedicated to my family

Nancy, Brady, Soojin, Malachi, Riley,
Clancy, Kara, Beatrice, Samuel
Colby, and Darren

And to America's Prosecutors

INTRODUCTION AND PREFACE

This short yet comprehensive *Handbook* is designed for both prosecutors and defense counsel alike. Its modest goal is to eradicate what is called "prosecutor misconduct." "Prosecutorial misconduct" or "prosecutor misconduct" is a misnomer. As is explained in Chapter 2, authors, lawyers, trial judges, appellate judges, academics, law professors, and others who should know better mislabel prosecutor behavior as "misconduct" when it clearly does not meet the definition of "misconduct."

Beyond aiming for truth in labeling, this *Handbook* is intended to serve as a guidebook for both prosecutors and defense counsel. It will assist prosecutors because it explains how to avoid committing those errors, which are commonly mislabeled as "misconduct", in pretrial and trial, and it will also aid defense counsel because it arms them with information that can be used to ensure that their clients receive a fair trial.

An example of how the *Handbook* simultaneously guides prosecutors and arms defense counsel is that it spells out what a prosecutor is prohibited by law and ethical rules from saying in trial. By identifying what a prosecutor is not permitted to say in trial, it not only tells prosecutors what not to do but also provides defense counsel with grounds and legal authority for either an objection, a motion for mistrial, or an appeal if the trial judge overrules the objection or denies the motion.

This *Handbook* is also intended for anyone who wants to understand the real roles and functions of the American prosecutor. Understanding the prosecutor's role is important because committing misconduct would be antithetical to a prosecutor's role and functions as a minister of justice. There is a wide-spread public misunderstanding (even among lawyers, law professors, and law students) of this role. This misconception is to a significant degree caused by movies, television shows, and books that cast prosecutors as antagonists in their narratives.

Eradicating American Prosecutor Misconduct traces the unique character of the American prosecutor from its origins to today because only by understanding that history can the roles and functions of a modern prosecutor be fully appreciated.

This *Handbook* is an outgrowth of Continuing Legal Education presentations on prosecutor professionalism that I delivered across the nation. It offers engaging and educational examples of prosecutor error along with the words from a cross-section of state and federal appellate courts describing both what and why certain prosecutorial conduct is prohibited. In sum, it offers learn-by-example lessons of what a prosecutor should not do in pretrial and trial.

IN THE BEGINNING

Disagreement exists about the origins of the American prosecutor's professionalism as we know it. Historians have traced the American prosecutor model back to either the English magistracy, the French office of public prosecutor (as a backlash against the English after the Revolution), the Dutch (the "schout" or "sheriff" in the Dutch colony of New Netherlands) or a mixture (the English private and police prosecution system coexisting alongside the Dutch public prosecution system). See *The Changing Role of the American Prosecutor*, John L. Worrall, Edited by John L. Worrall and M. Elaine Nugent-Borakove, State University of New York Press (2008) at 4.

Eventually, the colonies patterned their approach after the English system that had no public prosecutor. While, like the English, the American attorneys general could represent the Crown in both civil and criminal cases, most criminal prosecutions in the colonies were left up to the victim. However, this approach was ill-suited to the colonies because of the cost of prosecution, distances between settlements, and the ability of moneyed offenders to settle their cases. By the time of the American Revolution, each colony had adopted some system of public prosecution. When states were formed, county attorneys often prosecuted crimes under state law and city attorneys prosecuted crimes under town ordinances.

The Changing Role of the American Prosecutor, Id. at 5 describes the evolution of the prosecutor's role as follows:

> Prosecutors' current authority was not always in place, however. Throughout American history, the prosecutor evolved through several stages, from a weak figurehead to a powerful political figure. Jacoby (1980, p. 26) has identified four forces that have contributed to this progression. The first was political;

Americans chose a system of public instead of private prosecution. The second was legal; Americans pursuit of democracy begat local government systems. The third was an outgrowth of the second; prosecutors became elected (as opposed to appointed). Officials out of popular sentiment—consistent with democratic ideals. Finally, a desire to separate judicial and executive functions all but guaranteed an executive branch function for prosecutors.

Today, the American public prosecutorial model is in sharp contrast to its English counterpart. In criminal matters, the English Director of Public Prosecution is the Crown's solicitor who farms out the prosecution responsibility to Barristers who may on another day serve as defense counsel. At least one former Assistant District Attorney, Joseph Lawless, Jr. argues that the British private prosecutor approach is better because longevity in the American prosecutor post manifests itself in an "almost universal predilection to convict at all costs" and "breeds indifference to individual rights and cultivates only predisposition for conviction." *Prosecutorial Misconduct, Law and Procedure*, 4th ED, Joseph F. Lawless, Jr., Lexis Nexis (2021) at 5-6.

EARLY 20th CENTURY

To get a picture of the prosecutor's role in the early 1900s, consider a case that began in Caldwell, Idaho. On a snowy December 30, 1905, Idaho's former Governor Frank Steunenburg was walking towards his home in Caldwell. What happened next has been described as follows:

> Entering Sixteenth Avenue, he (Steunenburg) could see the lamplight burning behind the columns of his front porch the worm glow filtering through the lace curtains of his living room, where minutes before, Belle (his wife) and their two youngest children had knelt at their evening prayers. He reached down and pulled the wooden slide that opened the gate leading to his side door. As he turned to close it, an explosion split the evening calm, demolishing the gate, the eight-

inch-thick gatepost, and the nearby fencing, splintering yards of boardwalk, scooping a shallow oval hole in the frozen ground, and hurling the governor ten feet into his yard.

Big Trouble A Murder in a Small Western Town Sets Off a Struggle for the Soul of America, J. Anthony Lucas at 50, Simon and Shuster (1997)

Governor Frank Steunenburg

Governor Steunenburg's house with the gate shredded by the explosion

Steunenburg was assassinated because in 1899, when he was Governor, he had ended miner labor union (the Western Federation of Miners Union) violence in Northern Idaho by herding the miners into bullpens. Harry Orchard was one of the miners. He escaped and became the dynamiting assassin for the Federation who murdered opponents of the Federation in California, Colorado, and Idaho.

Orchard confessed to murdering Steunenburg, pled guilty and became a witness at the trial in Boise, Idaho of Big Bill Haywood, Secretary Treasurer of the Union, Charles Moyer, President of the Union, and G. A. Pettibone. At trial, Clarence Darrow, who later became a famous defense lawyer, represented these defendants.

What was the role of the prosecutor in America at the time of this turn-of-the-twentieth century trial? Who represented the state? Was the prosecutor a public official? Private attorney? In this Idaho case, the government was represented by O. M. Van Duyn, the elected prosecutor of Canyon County, William E. Borah, and chief special prosecutor James H. Hawley.

A reporter for the local newspaper, the *Statesman,* cornered Hawley and asked if he had "been retained as a private prosecutor in the interest of some individual or corporation." *Big Trouble*, supra at 353.

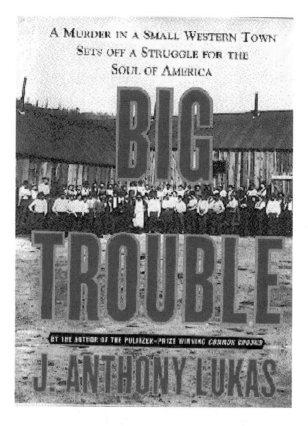

Big Trouble sheds light on the public versus private practice of prosecution at the time, as follows:

> Hawley responded as follows: "No Sir. I was retained by the state of Idaho to assist O. M. Van Duyn of Canyon County in the prosecution of these cases. I am not in the employ of any private individual or corporation. If such was the case, I would not hesitate to say so, for the statute provides that any private party or corporation interested in a prosecution of this nature may employ an attorney, providing the prosecuting attorney is willing to accept such assistance. I am, however, strictly in the employ of the state, and my retainer comes from no other source whatever.

Hawley's was the lawyer's answer, A shrewd blend of truth, obfuscation, and falsehood. The first sentence was arguably true: ostensibly, at least, Hawley had been hired to assist the inexperienced Owen Van Duyn of Canyon County—though in fact it was Van Duyn who served as junior assistant to Hawley and Borah. The second sentence was more problematic: on February 25, Hawley might justifiably deny that he was employed by a private party or corporation. But well before that date, he had relentlessly beaten the bushes for corporate contributors to the prosecution; he'd already flushed out some cash in the Coeur d'Alenes, with expectations of more to come: and he stood to benefit by $5000 if his salary was paid in whole, or in substantial part, from such contributions.

As for the legality of this practice, Hawley's claim that it was explicitly authorized by Idaho statute went beyond the facts. In 1906, there was no state statute that held, in Hawley's words, that "any private party or corporation interested in a prosecution of this nature may employ an attorney." The practice of hiring private counsel to assist prosecutors was an old one in the West, where it was rare to find competent prosecuting attorneys at the county level and where the mixture of public functions and private interest was endemic.

In 1884, a California court noted that the practice "has existed and been acquiesced in almost since the organization of the state." In two highly publicized cases pitting sheep men against cattlemen—the Diamond Field Jack case in Idaho, and the Spring Creek Raid in Wyoming—sheep men made no secret of hiring in and amply remunerating private attorneys to go after their sworn enemies, the cattleman and their agents. The more remote the locale, the more visible the case, the more potent the colliding forces and the more celebrated the defense attorneys, the more often another celebrated attorney would be called in to act for the prosecution—paid sometimes by the state, sometimes by an interested corporation or association. *Id.* at 353-354

In a footnote, *Big Trouble* states, "In Southern states, when a black man was charged with raping a white woman, it was long the practice for the family of the "victim", bent on revenge, to provide the 'prosecutor.'" (John P McKenzie, an interview with the author, October 1996).

Both Haywood and Pettibone were acquitted and the case against Moyer was dismissed.

In 1987, the United States Supreme Court declared that private counsel serving as an American prosecutor may not have a direct interest in the outcome. *Young v. United States ex rel Vuitton et Fils S.A.*, 107 S. Ct. 2124, 2136 (1987). Nevertheless, a state may recognize the common law right of a victim or the victim's family to assist the public prosecutor, but the assisting counsel has a limited role. *Price v. Commonwealth*, 849 S. E. 140, 146 (2020) explains:

> Nevertheless, Virginia recognizes the "common-law right of a crime victim, or of his family, to assist the prosecution with privately employed counsel." *Cantrell*, 229 Va. at 392, 329 S.E.2d 22. The overarching principle governing the private prosecutor's participation is that "the public prosecutor must remain in continuous control of the case." *Id.* at 393, 329 S.E.2d 22. Limits on the private prosecutor's authority ensure that the participation of a private prosecutor is only supplemental to the elected official's handling of the case. The private prosecutor "may not initiate a prosecution or appear before the grand jury." Id. He may appear in the case "only by the leave of the trial court ... [and] may participate only with the express consent of the public prosecutor."4 *Id.*

The private prosecutor may make a closing argument
to the jury only if the court, in its discretion, permits
it; and the private prosecutor , likewise, may not
participate in plea bargaining or in "a decision to
accept a plea of guilty to a lesser crime or to enter
a *nolle prosequi.*" *Id.* These procedural safeguards
protect the defendant's due process right to the fair-
minded exercise of the Commonwealth's attorney's
discretion. *Lux*, 24 Va. App. at 569-70, 484 S.E.2d
145.

When privately employed counsel assists
the prosecutor, moreover, he takes on the higher
ethical obligations of the prosecutor. *Cantrell*, 229
Va. at 393, 329 S.E.2d 22. Just as the
public prosecutor may not entertain divided loyalties
between the interests of justice and the interests of a
private client, neither may the
private prosecutor attempt the same. "[T]he
private prosecutor is prohibited ... from advocating
any cause which would be forbidden to the
public prosecutor " *Id.*; see also *Young*, 481 U.S. at
804, 107 S. Ct. at 2136 ("A private attorney appointed
to prosecute a criminal contempt therefore certainly
should be as disinterested as a public prosecutor who
undertakes such a prosecution.").

All persons who hold the "distinctive role" given
to prosecutors, *Young*, 481 U.S. at 803, 107 S. Ct. at
2135–36, whether for the duration of one case or for a
term of office, must maintain the impartiality befitting
the system of justice. In short, if it is forbidden to the
public prosecutor it is forbidden to the
private prosecutor.

Currently, the American prosecutor is a public figure with a central
role in the criminal justice system. However, as William F. McDonald
notes, "Today prosecutors have an extensive domain and are regarded

as potentially, if not in reality, the key actor in the criminal justice system. But, this is a comparatively recent development. In the older big cities, it is less than 100 years old." William F. McDonald, *The Prosecutor* at p. 19, Sage Publications (1979).

1935 – THE PROSECUTOR'S ROLE DEFINED—*BERGER V. UNITED STATES*
"guilt shall not escape nor innocence suffer"

In 1935, the United States Supreme Court defined the role of the prosecutor in America. The *Berger v. United States* decision has been adopted and cited by appellate courts across the nation. Justice Sutherland's often-quoted words describing the prosecutor's role are these:

> "The United States Attorney is the representative not of an ordinary party to a controversy, but of a sovereignty whose obligation to govern impartially is as compelling as its obligation to govern at all; and whose interest, therefore, in a criminal prosecution is not that it shall win a case but that justice shall be done. As such, he is in a peculiar and very definite sense the servant of the law, the twofold aim of which is that guilt shall not escape nor innocence suffer. He may prosecute with earnestness and vigor—indeed, he should do so. But, while he may strike hard blows, he is not at liberty to strike foul ones. It is as much his duty to refrain from improper methods calculated to produce a wrongful conviction as it is to use every legitimate means to bring about a just one."
> *Berger v. United States*, 295 U.S. 78 (1935).

The *Berger* decision has been cited in federal appellate courts, such as in *Stermer v. Warren*, 959 F.3d 704, 725 (2020), and in state after state appellate courts when called upon to define or reflect on the prosecutor's role. An example of a state appellate court pointing to *Berger* as the guiding light is *Price v. Commonwealth, supra.* at p. 145 (2020), which held as follows:

It has been said that "[t]he prosecutor has more control over life, liberty, and reputation than any other person in America." Robert H. Jackson, Att'y Gen. of the U.S., The Federal Prosecutor, Address to the Second Annual Conference of United States Attorneys (Apr. 1, 1940). The prosecutor's great power carries with it great ethical obligations. *Young v. U.S. ex rel. Vuitton et Fils S.A.*, 481 U.S. 787, 803, 107 S. Ct. 2124, 2135–36, 95 L.Ed.2d 740 (1987) (recognizing that the prosecutor has a "distinctive role" in the criminal justice system).

The prosecutor is "a sovereignty whose obligation to govern impartially is as compelling as its obligation to govern at all; and whose interest, therefore, in a criminal prosecution is not that it shall win a case, but that justice shall be done." *Id.* (quoting *Berger v. United States*, 295 U.S. 78, 88, 55 S.Ct. 629, 633, 79 L.Ed.1314 (1935)). As a "minister of justice," Va. R. of Prof. Conduct 3.8 cmt. 1, the prosecutor's "duty is to seek justice, not merely to convict," *Young*, 481 U.S. at 803, 107 S. Ct. at 135–36 (quoting Model Code of Prof. Resp.EC 7-13 (Am. Bar Ass'n 1982)).

This role as a minister of justice carries with it high ethical obligations and a duty of impartiality. A Commonwealth's attorney has duties to conduct "the impartial prosecution" of the accused and to ensure that the accused receives a fair trial. *Lux v. Commonwealth*, 24 Va. App. 561, 568, 484 S.E.2d 145 (1997). The prosecutor is "obligat[ed] to see that the defendant is accorded procedural justice and that guilt is decided upon the basis of sufficient evidence." Va. R. of Prof. Conduct 3.8 cmt. 1. The prosecutor is ultimately accountable not to any victim but to justice.

Another example of a state's high court citing *Berger* is South Carolina's Supreme Court. In *State v. Dawkins*, 297 S.C. 386, 377 S.E. 2d 299 (1988), South Carolina's Supreme Court described the case under consideration as "a prime example of a prosecutor striving to obtain a conviction regardless of costs, only to have the conviction reduced to vulnerability because of the improper tactics." Then, the Supreme Court "caution(ed) prosecutors throughout this state to be mindful of the words of Mr. Justice Sutherland. . . (the above-quoted language in *Berger)*." The *Berger* doctrine has been cited with approval in other South Carolina cases. *State v. Robinson*, 4098 S.E.2d 404, 410(1991), and *State v. Davis*, 122 S.E.2d 633, 635(1961).

Berger Codified—"Minister of Justice"

The *Berger* doctrine was codified into Model Rule of Professional Conduct 3.8. The commentary to Rule 3.8 explains:

> A prosecutor has the responsibility of a minister of justice and not simply that of an advocate. This responsibility carries with it specific obligations to see that the defendant is accorded procedural justice, that guilt is decided upon the basis of sufficient evidence, and that special precautions are taken to prevent and to rectify the conviction of innocent persons.

Rule 3.8 provides:

> The prosecutor in a criminal case shall:
>
> (a) refrain from prosecuting a charge that the prosecutor knows is not supported by probable cause;
>
> (b) make reasonable efforts to assure that the accused has been advised of the right to, and the procedure for obtaining, counsel and has been given reasonable opportunity to obtain counsel;

(c) not seek to obtain from an unrepresented accused a waiver of important pretrial rights, such as the right to a preliminary hearing;

(d) make timely disclosure to the defense of all evidence or information known to the prosecutor that tends to negate the guilt of the accused or mitigates the offense, and, in connection with sentencing, disclose to the defense and to the tribunal all unprivileged mitigating information known to the prosecutor, except when the prosecutor is relieved of this responsibility by a protective order of the tribunal;

(e) not subpoena a lawyer in a grand jury or other criminal proceeding to present evidence about a past or present client unless the prosecutor reasonably believes:

(1) the information sought is not protected from disclosure by any applicable privilege;

(2) the evidence sought is essential to the successful completion of an ongoing investigation or prosecution; and

(3) there is no other feasible alternative to obtain the information;

(f) except for statements that are necessary to inform the public of the nature and extent of the prosecutor's action and that serve a legitimate law enforcement purpose, refrain from making extrajudicial comments that have a substantial likelihood of heightening public condemnation of the accused and exercise reasonable care to prevent investigators, law enforcement personnel, employees or other persons assisting or associated with the prosecutor in a criminal case from making an extrajudicial statement that the prosecutor would be prohibited from making under Rule 3.6 or this Rule.

(g) When a prosecutor knows of new, credible and material evidence creating a reasonable likelihood that a convicted defendant did not commit an offense of which the defendant was convicted, the prosecutor shall:

(1) promptly disclose that evidence to an appropriate court or authority, and

(2) if the conviction was obtained in the prosecutor's jurisdiction,

(i) promptly disclose that evidence to the defendant unless a court authorizes delay, and

(ii) undertake further investigation, or make reasonable efforts to cause an investigation, to determine whether the defendant was convicted of an offense that the defendant did not commit.

(h) When a prosecutor knows of clear and convincing evidence establishing that a defendant in the prosecutor's jurisdiction was convicted of an offense that the defendant did not commit, the prosecutor shall seek to remedy the conviction.

Higher Standard

People v. Hill, 17 Cal.4th 800, 72 Cal. Rptr.2d 656 (1998) cites *Berger* and states: "Prosecutors, however, are held to an elevated standard of conduct. . . A prosecutor is held to a standard higher than that imposed on other attorneys because of the unique function he or she performs in representing the interests, and exercising the sovereign power of the State." 72 Cal. Rptr. 665.

By Contrast to Defense Counsel

Defense counsel shall act accordingly "regardless of what he (sic) thinks or knows to be the truth." This sharp contrast puts the prosecutor's role in perspective. *United States v. Wade,* 388 U.S. 256 (1967) held as follows:

> Law enforcement officers have the obligation to convict the guilty and to make sure they do not convict the innocent. They must be dedicated to making the criminal trial a procedure for the ascertainment of the true facts surrounding the commission of the crime. To this extent, our so-called adversary system is not adversary at all; nor should it be. But, defense counsel has no comparable obligation to ascertain or present the truth.

> Our system assigns him a different mission. He must be and is interested in preventing the conviction of the innocent, but, absent a voluntary plea of guilty, we must also insist that he defend his client whether he is innocent or guilty. The state has the obligation to present the evidence. He need not present any witnesses to the police, or reveal any confidences of his client, or furnish any other information to help the prosecutor's case. If he can confuse a witness, even a truthful one, or make him appear at a disadvantage, unsure or indecisive, that will be his normal course.

> Our interest in not convicting the innocent permits counsel to put the State to its proof, to put the State's case in the worst possible light, regardless of what he thinks or knows to be the truth."

Imitation is Misconduct

Noted defense counsel, law professor and author Alan Dershowitz offered his explanation of why some prosecutors have departed from the role laid out for prosecutors in the *Berger* decision and Model Rule of Professional Responsibility 3.8, as follows:

It is far easier for a prosecutor to rationalize engaging in questionable conduct when he knows that the defense attorney—his opponent in the adversarial process—is entirely free to engage in analogous behavior. And therein lies the key—in my view—to *why* prosecutors engage in misconduct. They often find it difficult to understand why defense attorneys are free to do things that they are forbidden to do.

On a more subtle—yet perhaps equally important—level prosecutors often fail to notice that they are coming close to the line, because defense attorneys go so far over the same analogous line. . .

One of the primary reasons why otherwise honest prosecutors engage in certain kinds of misbehavior can be summarized in two words: "defense attorneys.'..."

Alan Dershowitz's Foreward to *Prosecutorial Misconduct*, J. Lawless, Kluwer Law Book Publ., N.Y., N.Y. (1985).

The phrase "prosecutor misconduct" or "prosecutorial misconduct" is a commonly used phrase. Without care, authors use it as titles for their books—an Amazon search will pop up over a half dozen books titled *Prosecutorial Misconduct* including Joseph F. Lawless's fourth edition of *Prosecutorial Misconduct.* Lawyers, trial judges, appellate judges, academics, law professors, Innocence Projects, and others who should know better indiscriminately misapply the label. Let's stop and think about truth in labeling.

The word "misconduct" has nasty connotations. "Misconduct" is defined by the Merriam-Webster dictionary as "intentional or wanton wrongful but usually not criminal behavior, as: deliberate or wanton violation of standards of conduct by a government official." When referring to alleged prosecutorial error, some appellate courts have elevated the prosecutor's conduct to that tantamount to criminal behavior. For instance, *State v. Campbell*, 23 P.3d 176, 181 (2001), observed, "The question of whether a particular prosecutor has been *guilty of misconduct* in the trial of a criminal case is the subject of some relatively controversial recent decisions by our Supreme Court and by this court. . . ." (Emphasis added).

The Texas District and County Attorney's Association issued a report in 2012 entitled "Setting the Record Straight on Prosecutorial Misconduct" (online at www.tdcaa.com/reports/setting-the-record-straight-on-prosecutor-misconduct) in which it specifically offered a definition of "prosecutorial misconduct" and an explanation as follows:

> The American Bar Associations sees this issue as so fundamental that in 2010, its House of Delegates passed ABA Resolution 100B urging, "trial and appellate courts, in criminal cases, when reviewing the conduct of prosecutors to differentiate between 'error' and 'prosecutorial misconduct.'" The

comment to the resolution explains that "[a] finding of prosecutorial misconduct may be perceived as reflecting intentional wrongdoing, or even professional misconduct, even in cases where such a perception is entirely unwarranted, and this resolution is directed at this perception.

To elevate the Innocence Project's claims of prosecutorial misconduct for the purpose of identifying serious conduct that is not being adequately prevented or sanctioned, the subcommittee did what the Innocence Project avoided—it developed a definition of the term:

> Prosecutorial misconduct occurs when a prosecutor deliberately engages in dishonest or fraudulent conduct calculated to produce an unjust result.

The working definition is not offered as a legal definition by which to judge whether a conviction or sentence should be overturned, but is merely intended to help identify the type of underhanded or dishonest action that the public would commonly identify as "misconduct." For that reason the definition contemplates that actions be deliberate, but it excludes common trial errors and minor mistakes made in good faith.

Using this definition, the subcommittee analyzed the claims made by the Innocence Project and concluded that its claims of prosecutor misconduct in Texas were vastly overstated.

When trial judges commit trial errors, appellate courts would never consider finding the trial judges guilty of "judicial misconduct." How receptive would an appellate court bench be to an argument that the trial judge committed "trial judge misconduct" when the allegation refers to trial error by the judge (such as, overruling a proper objection, delivering a faulty jury instruction), rather than the judge's bad or dishonest conduct. Also, it is ironic that an appellate court would rule that a prosecutor is "guilty of prosecutorial misconduct" for using a pejorative term during closing argument to describe a defendant's conduct. Just as a judge's trial error would not be called "misconduct," prosecutors should receive the same courtesy.

"Trial error" is a more apt description for all but the few cases where the prosecutor's conduct actually meets the definition of "misconduct." In that regard, this *Handbook* recommends putting an end to use of the phrase "prosecutorial misconduct."

But more significantly, this *Handbook* explores significant areas of vulnerability for prosecutorial error that appellate courts have considered under the rubric "prosecutorial misconduct," and it offers ways to make sure no prosecutorial error is committed. *No matter what the label is, prosecutorial "error" or "misconduct," prosecutors, who are devoted to their role as ministers of justice, want none of it.*

CONSEQUENCES OF PROSECUTOR ERROR

The consequences that can flow from a prosecutor's commission of trial error can be dire not only for the defendant but also for the prosecutor. For the prosecutor, the consequences can range from a judicial admonition to the prosecutor, loss of the government's case, and loss of a bar license. Here those consequences are examined because knowledge of what the consequences of trial error can be is the best incentive to avoid error.

Sending a Message to the Prosecutor

Even when the appellate court holds that the prosecutorial behavior does not warrant reversal of the conviction, it may send its message to the prosecutor's office. Judge Joseph Anderson, Jr., in his book titled, *The Lost Art – An Advocate's Guide to Effective Closing Argument,* at page 81, put it this way: ". . . Finally, the appellate courts have occasionally issued paradoxical rulings, telling the prosecutor, in effect 'it's not error, but don't ever do it again.'"

For instance, in *United States v. Moore*, 11 F.3d 475, 482(4th Cir. 1993), the court described the prosecutor's argument as ". . . improper and indicative of a shoddy and somewhat paltry closing argument" and in *State v. Dawkins*, 377 S.E. 2d 299 (S.C. 1988), South Carolina's Supreme Court described the prosecutor's conduct as "a prime example of a prosecutor striving to obtain a conviction regardless of costs, only to have the conviction reduced to vulnerability because of the improper tactics." Or, even more directly in *State v. Primus*, 535 S.E.2d 152, 157 (2000), ". . . We take this opportunity to strenuously caution members of the Bar, particularly attorneys for the State, to carefully tailor their arguments within constitutional guidelines and restrictions."

In *State v. Price*, 948 P.2d 1145, 1148, 24 Kan. App. 580 (1997), the Kansas Court of Appeals sent this message:

> We are deeply concerned with the content and tenor
> of the statements made by the Dickenson County
> Attorney during closing argument. The statements
> that we have noted in this opinion were improper and
> beyond the limit of zealous and robust advocacy. . .

Likewise, in *People v. Herrero*, 756 N.E.2d 234, 245, 324 Ill. App. 3d 876 (2001), the Appellate Court of Illinois, First District, Fifth Division held:

> For prosecutor Hughes to have commented on
> Herrero's decision to exercise his constitutional right
> to a jury is outrageous, casting a shadow over the
> proceedings that simply cannot be ignored. . .

Illinois appellate courts are not supposed to use reversals for deterrence reasons, and this has troubled them. In *People v. Parchman*, 707 N.E. 88, 94, 302 Ill. App.3d 27 (1998), the Appellate Court of Illinois, First District, Fifth Division observed:

Upon review of the record and upon reluctant realization that we do not send a meaningful message to the overzealous prosecutor, we hold that the error was harmless in this case. Courts of review are often faced with the dilemma of how to send a message to the overzealous prosecutor without reversing an otherwise fair and appropriate trial.

However, at least one appellate Justice decided that reversal had been used as a deterrent message. In *People v. Derr*, 736 N.E. 693,700, 316 Ill. App. 3d 272 (2000), Justice Welch of the Illinois Appellate Court, Fifth District dissented holding as follows:

In *United States v Hasting*, 461 U.S. 499, 76 L.Ed. 2d 96, 103 S.Ct. 1974 (1983), the United States Supreme Court held that a court may not use reversal of a criminal conviction as a means to punish or deter perceived prosecutorial misconduct in closing argument where the improper argument amounts to harmless error. In the instant case, the majority has disregarded the Supreme Court's admonition. The prosecutor's closing argument in the case at bar, even if improper, amounts to no more than harmless error and does not warrant reversal of defendant's conviction. Accordingly, I dissent.

Mistrial, Dismissal, and Double Jeopardy

People v. Walker, 720 N.E.2d 297, 308 Ill. App.3d 435 (1999) serves as a good example of not only the possible consequences of a trial motion for mistrial and double jeopardy attaching when prosecutorial error is alleged but also how to effectively respond to the allegation of misconduct. In this criminal sexual assault trial, the prosecutor told the detective that the State's motion in limine had been denied and therefore the detective could not discuss defendant's prior sexual assaults.

Nevertheless, the detective on direct gave a nonresponsive answer to the Assistant State's Attorney's question, inserting a reference to the defendant's past sexually violent behavior. The detective ignored the court's ruling sustaining the defense objection and instruction to the jury to disregard the detective's statements and mentioned the defendant's record again.

Defense counsel moved for a mistrial. The prosecutor took effective action by testifying about her admonition to the detective. Defense counsel claimed that statements by the detective should be imputed to the prosecutor, that they amounted to overreaching and that retrial should be barred. *Walker*, 720 N.E.2d at 300 noted that prosecutorial misconduct by overreaching may result in a double jeopardy bar, as follows:

> However, an exception to this general rule arises when the defendant's conviction resulted from prosecutorial overreaching. *People v. Brown*, 222 Ill. App. 3d 703, 711, 165 Ill. Dec. 176, 584 N.E.2d 355 (1991). The definition of prosecutorial overreaching is "prosecutorial misconduct specifically designed to cause or provoke a mistrial in order to obtain a second, more favorable opportunity to convict the accused." *Brown*, 222 Ill. App. 3d at 711.

> Prosecutorial misconduct also arises when the prosecutor's conduct is "motivated by bad faith to harass or prejudice the accused." *Brown*, 222 Ill. App. 3d at 711. In order for double jeopardy to attach in a case where the prosecution has harassed the defendant or overreached its authority, it must be shown that the prosecution intended to subvert the protections that are guaranteed under the double jeopardy clause. *Oregon v. Kennedy*, 456 U.S. 667, 675-76, 72 L.Ed.2d 416, 424, 102 S. Ct. 2083, 2089 (1982).

The Appellate Court in *Walker*, 720 N.E.2d at 301 found that the record contained no evidence that the State's Attorney "in the slightest way" was involved in eliciting the improper testimony and went on to hold:

> Allowing a police officer's inappropriate trial
> testimony, without collusion by the prosecutor's
> office, to bind the State on double jeopardy principles
> would infringe on the State's Attorney's independent
> power to decide whether or not to prosecute a
> defendant for an offense. We believe that imputing a
> police officer's comments to the State and holding
> that double jeopardy attaches, in the absence of
> prosecutorial misconduct, when a police officer
> testifies about explicitly excluded evidence would
> take away the unique authority to prosecute offenders
> that is granted to the State's Attorney.

Reversal—"Do It Right or, Do It Again

David P. Harris, Sr. Deputy District Attorney,
Stanislaus County, CA.

Regarding frequency of prosecutorial error, *Understanding
Reversible Error in Criminal Appeals*, Final Report Submitted to the
State Justice Institute by the National Center for State Courts. (Joy
Chapper and Roger Hanson, Co-Project Directors) (1989) found the
following:

Frequency of issue on appeal. The following issues are addressed on
appeal in the following percentages of cases. (The total exceeds
100% because some cases involve more than one issue.).

Evidentiary Ruling   43.0%
Sufficiency of Evidence 35.1%
Jury Instructions   29.5%
Sentence/sentencing hearing 24.5%
Suppression of evidence or statements 14.5%
Prosecutorial Misconduct   12.7%
Judicial intrusion or management 9.7%
Jury selection or deliberation 7.9%
Suppression of identification/line-up 6.2%
Lesser included offenses/merger 3.5%

Speedy trial   3.3%
Statutory Interpretation 1.2%
Constitutionality of statute 1.0%

Error rates and reversal rates. The same study indicated that certain kinds of issues led to a finding of error in certain percentages of cases, and to reversal in certain percentages of cases. Those figures are in column one—the Issue, column 2—the percentage of all errors associated with the issue and in column 3—the reversal rate:

Issue	% of errors	Reversal rate
Admission/exclusion of evidence	20.6%	7.7%
Instructions	13.5%	9.7%
Procedural/discretionary ruling	13.1%	7.8%
Sufficiency of evidence	12.0%	5.8%
Merger of offenses	10.5%	51.9%
Suppression (evid/ID/statement)	10.5%	8.4%
Ineffective/waiver of counsel	6.0%	12.9%
Other constitutional claims	4.9%	11.5%
Jury selection/deliberations	3.4%	8.8%
Statutory interp/application	2.2%	19.4%
Voluntaries of plea	2.2%	15.0%
Prosecutorial misconduct	***1.1%***	***1.9%***

Based on the data, prosecutorial error resulted in a relatively small percentage of convictions being overturned. But, even if less than two percent were found to have been caused by prosecutorial error, that is still too many cases.

Disciplinary Proceedings

Under Rule of Professional Conduct 8.4, Misconduct, "It is professional misconduct for a lawyer to violate the Model Rules of Professional Conduct, knowingly assist or induce another to do so, or do so through the acts of another."

In the Matter of John Lloyd Swarts, III, 30 P.3d 1011 (KS 2001) is illustrative of what can happen if a prosecutor errs at trial. In

Swarts, a disciplinary panel issued a 26-page report of findings of fact and conclusions of law regarding the conduct of the Bourbon County Attorney concerning improprieties including improper cross-examination and closing argument. Based upon its findings and conclusions, the Hearing Panel recommended that the Respondent be suspended from the practice of law for a year. The Kansas Supreme Court, after finding clear and convincing evidence of various ethical violations, permitted the County Attorney to serve as Bourbon County Attorney until January 1, 2002, and to resign when eligible for retirement benefits and retire from the practice of law and go inactive status at that time.

Civil Liability

Civil liability of the prosecutor is an unlikely consequence of prosecutorial misconduct because a prosecutor is almost completely immune from civil liability. In *Imbler v. Pachtman*, 424 U.S. 409 (1976), the United States Supreme Court held that prosecutors were absolutely immune for their actions that were "intimately associated with the judicial phase of the criminal process." The Court noted that effective checks on the prosecutor aside from civil liability included possible criminal prosecution for willful acts and professional discipline. In *Imbler*, the prosecutor had wrongfully initiated the case, knowingly introduced false testimony at trial, and withheld exculpatory evidence from the defense, all in violation of the plaintiff's constitutional rights.

POWER OF THE PROSECUTOR

How powerful is the American prosecutor? Emily Bazelon in her book *Charged: The New Movement to Transform American Prosecution and End Mass Incarceration* places blame for mass incarceration at the feet of America's prosecutors, stating:

> The unfettered power of prosecutors is the missing piece for explaining how the number of people incarcerated in the United States has *quadrupled* since the 1980s, to a total of almost 2.2 million. Our level of imprisonment is five to ten times higher than that of other liberal democracies—nine times Germany's and seven times France's. There's more: when the system misfires in the worst way possible, by convicting an innocent person, a prosecutor's errors or, less frequently, willful misconduct often account for the breakdown, at least in part. And when black defendants are punished more severely than white defendants for similar crimes, the choices of prosecutors are largely to blame. Though they're not the only ones at fault, their decisions are the ones that matter most of all.
>
> Emily Bazelon, *Charged: The New Movement to Transform American Prosecution and End Mass Incarceration* (Random House 2019) at xxv.

On the other hand, Bazelon describes prosecutors as having the power to eradicate mass incarceration, as follows:

> Here's the thing: prosecutors also hold the key to change. They can protect against convicting the innocent. They can guard against racial bias. They can curtail mass incarceration.

Change who occupies the prosecutor's office, and you can make the system begin to operate differently. The power of the D.A. makes him or her the actor—the only actor—who can start to fix what's broken without changing a single law.

Id. at xxvi

CHARGING DECISION

The authority to make charging decisions makes the prosecutor a commanding player in the criminal justice system. A prosecutor decides whether or not criminal charges should be filed and what crime or crimes should be charged. Those decisions affect human lives, the administration of justice, and the community as a whole.

Constitutional Limitations

The prosecutor's exercise of discretion in charging some but not others with the same crime does not violate the equal protection clause of the federal constitution if it was not "deliberately based upon an unjustifiable standard such as race, religion, or other arbitrary classification." *Oyler v. Boles*, 368 U.S. 448, 456, 82 S. Ct. 501 (1962).

Model Rules of Professional Conduct: Probable Cause

The model rules of professional conduct impose only minimal standards on prosecutors for filing criminal charges. Model Rule of Professional Conduct 3.8(a) states, "The prosecutor in a criminal case shall: (a) refrain from prosecuting a charge that the prosecutor knows is not supported by probable cause." Probable cause is defined as having reasonable grounds to believe that a crime has been committed and that the person committed the crime. This is a low bar, and if prosecutors filed charges whenever there was probable cause to believe a crime was committed and that a person committed the crime, the criminal justice system would be overwhelmed.

Prosecutor Filing and Disposition Standards

A national movement in the 1970s pushed for the adoption of prosecutorial standards to govern the exercise of discretion in making filing and disposition decisions. State statutes have been enacted that recommend the adoption of prosecutor filing and disposition standards. For example, the Revised Code of Washington 13.40.077 recommend prosecuting standards for charging and plea dispositions in the state of Washington.

PRETRIAL PUBLICITY

Sheppard v. Maxwell

The seminal case governing today's pretrial publicity in criminal cases is *Sheppard v. Maxwell*, 384 U.S. 333, 86 S. Ct. 1507 (1966). Dr. Sam Sheppard was accused of murdering his wife, Marilyn.

In 1954, Dr. Sam Sheppard was 29 and a neurosurgeon who made $33,000 a year. He lived in a white frame house on the shore of Lake Erie. During the night, Sam Sheppard's wife Marilyn was beaten around the head until her head was a bloody pulp. Sam Sheppard claimed he slept on the couch downstairs and was awakened by his wife's screams. He said when he went upstairs, a bushy headed man who was six foot two inches tall ran towards him, pushed him aside, and fled.

Dr. Sheppard was charged with murder. Some of the evidence included: no signs of forced entry; Sheppard's t-shirt had disappeared; a bag with Sheppard's watch and ring were discovered at the house; and he was having an affair with a lab technician. Sheppard was convicted.

After seven years in prison, Sheppard got a new lawyer F. Lee Bailey, who was described as a "young, unknown and inexperienced lawyer from Boston." That Boston lawyer, who would later in his career represent O.J. Simpson in the trial for murdering his wife Nicole Brown Simpson, carried Sheppard's case through the federal system to the United States Supreme Court. Bailey's theory was that his client had been denied due process by the media and that the trial judge failed to exercise control. He was successful in convincing the Supreme Court to render a landmark decision.

The 184-page Supreme-Court opinion granting a new trial states:

> Reporters were seated inside the bar, which made confidential talk among Sheppard and his counsel almost impossible during the proceedings. During recesses pictures were taken in the courtroom and newsmen even handled and photographed trial exhibits laying on the counsel table.
>
> . . . Even though each juror indicated that he could render an impartial verdict despite the prejudicial newspaper articles, we set aside the conviction. . .

The Supreme Court held that when trial publicity creates a probability of prejudice to the defendant, the defendant is denied due process of law if the trial judge does not take steps sufficient to ensure a fair trial for the defendant.

The case was retried. Bailey contended that the blood spatter showed that the killer was left-handed, and the killer could not have been Sam Sheppard because Sheppard was right-handed. Sheppard was acquitted.

F. Lee Bailey

The Fugitive, first a television show and later a movie starring Harrison Ford, were undoubtedly loosely inspired by the fact pattern of *Sheppard v. Maxwell.* The television series ran from 1963 until 1967 when the fugitive was exonerated. The last episode was the highest rated program on television—72% of the television audience watched it. In the television and movie versions, the man being chased was Sam Girard.

Protection Against Prejudicial Pretrial Publicity Codified

The Model Rule of Professional Conduct 3.6(a) and (d) is designed to prevent prejudicial pretrial publicity, stating that a "lawyer shall not make an extrajudicial statement that a reasonable person would expect to be disseminated by means of public communication if the lawyer knows or reasonably should know that it will have a substantial likelihood of materially prejudicing an adjudicative proceeding."

Rule 3.6(b) enumerates these statements as being permissible:

(1)   the claim, offense or defense involved and, except when prohibited by law, the identity of the persons involved;

(2)   information contained in a public record;

(3)   that an investigation of a matter is in progress;

(4)   the scheduling or result of any step in litigation;

(5)   a request for assistance in obtaining evidence and information necessary thereto;

(6)   a warning of danger concerning the behavior of a person involved, when there is reason to believe that there exists the likelihood of substantial harm to an individual or to the public interest; and

(7)   in a criminal case, in addition to subparagraphs (1) through (6):

      (i)   the identity, residence, occupation and family status of the accused;

      (ii)   if the accused has not been apprehended, information necessary to aid in apprehension of that person;

      (iii)   the fact, time and place of arrest;

      (iv)   the identity of investigating and arresting officers or agencies and the length of the investigation.

Comments to Rule 3.6 describe these subjects as "more likely than not to have a material prejudicial effect on a proceeding, particularly when they refer to . . . a criminal matter, or any other proceedings that could result in incarceration:"

(1)   the character, credibility, reputation or criminal record of a party, suspect in a criminal investigation or witness, or the identity of a witness, or the expected testimony of a party or witness;

(2)   in a criminal proceeding that could result in incarceration, the possibility of a plea of guilty to the offense or the existence or contents of any confession, admission, or statement given by a defendant or suspect or that person's refusal or failure to make a statement;

(3)   the performance or results of any examination or test or the refusal or failure of a person to submit to an examination or test, or the identity or nature of physical evidence expected to

be presented;

(4)   any opinion as to the guilt or innocence of a defendant or suspect in a criminal case or proceeding that could result in incarceration;

(5)   information that the lawyer knows or reasonably should know is likely to be inadmissible as evidence in a trial and that would, if disclosed, create a substantial risk of prejudicing an impartial trial; or

(6)   the fact that a defendant has been charged with a crime, unless there is included therein a statement explaining that the charge is merely an accusation and that the defendant is presumed innocent until and unless proven guilty.

Responsibility for Extrajudicial Statements by Others in the Prosecution Team

Model Rule of Professional Responsibility 3.6 states that the prosecutor shall "exercise reasonable care to prevent investigators, law enforcement personnel, employees or other persons assisting or associated with the prosecutor in a criminal case from making an extrajudicial statement that the prosecutor would be prohibited from making under Rule 3.6."

PLEA NEGOTIATIONS

Originally a Judicial Function

In 1804, one of the first American guilty pleas was entered. By 1839, about 24% of the convictions in New York were by guilty pleas. By 1860, that percentage had doubled. In 1929, 90% of all the convictions in New York were by guilty plea.

Plea negotiation was once a judicial function. Bargaining in the 1940s has been described as follows:

> . . .the story was pretty much the same. Judges either engaged in implicit bargaining or played active roles in negotiating with defendants for guilty pleas. In St.

Louis they referred to it as "burning the black candle."
Judges negotiated directly with defendants in their
chambers. In New York judges simply warned
defendants that if they pled guilty they would get
mercy whereas if they went to trial they would get
justice."
The Prosecutor, supra, at 29.

Nature of the Bargaining

The United States Supreme Court has stated, "But in the `give and
take' of plea bargaining, there is no such element of punishment or
retaliation so long as the accused is free to accept or reject the
prosecution's offer." *Bordenkircher v. Hayes,* 434 U.S. 357 (1977).

The Negotiated Contract

The bargain is a contract that the prosecutor is bound to keep. In the
key case, *Santobello v. New York*, 404 U.S. 257, 92 S. Ct. 495 (1971),
the prosecutor mistakenly made a recommendation for the maximum
sentence even though the prior prosecutor promised to make no
recommendation. The United States Supreme Court remanded the
case for a hearing to decide whether to resentence or allow a plea
withdrawal. The Court held that this measure was necessary to
preserve the integrity of the plea-bargaining process and stated,
"(T)his is in no sense to question the fairness of the sentencing judge;
the fault here rests on the prosecutor, not on the sentencing judge."
Santobello, supra at 263.

DISCOVERY

Brady v. Maryland

Brady v. Maryland, 373 U.S. 83, 83 S. Ct. 1194 (1963) involved a
prosecution for murder where the defendant requested records of
extrajudicial statements of the defendant's accomplice in which the
accomplice admitted committing the murder. The Supreme Court
held:

We now hold that the suppression by the prosecution of evidence favorable to an accused upon request violates due process where the evidence is material either to guilt or to punishment, irrespective of the good faith or bad faith of the prosecution.

(This principle) is not punishment of society for misdeeds of a prosecutor but avoidance of an unfair trial to the accused. Society wins not only when the guilty are convicted but when criminal trials are fair; our system of the administration of justice suffers when any accused is treated unfairly. An inscription on the walls of the Department of Justice states the proposition candidly for the federal domain: `The United States wins its point whenever justice is done its citizens in the court.'

A prosecution that withholds evidence on demand of an accused which, if made available, would tend to exculpate him or reduce the penalty helps shape a trial that bears heavily on the defendant. That casts the prosecutor in the role of an architect of a proceeding that does not comport with standards of justice, even though, as in the present case, his action is not `the result of guile,' to use the words of the Court of Appeals." *Brady,* 373 U.S. at 87-88.

Brady Codified

Model Rules of Professional Conduct 3.8(d) codify the *Brady* doctrine as follow:

The prosecutor in a criminal case shall make timely disclosure to the defense of all evidence or information known to the prosecutor that tends to negate the guilt of the accused or mitigates the offense, and, in connection with sentencing, disclose to the defense and to the tribunal all unprivileged mitigating information known to the prosecutor, except when the prosecutor is relieved of this responsibility by a protective order of the tribunal.

Consequences of a *Brady* Violations

Are the consequences of a *Brady* violation serious, and if so, how serious? The Senator Theodore Steven's case serves as an example of how bad they can be.

Ted Stevens served as Alaska's Senator from 1968 to 2010. In 2008, a federal grand jury indicted Senator Stevens for seven counts of failing to properly disclose gifts, which is a felony. He was alleged to have not disclosed renovations to his home and alleged gifts from VECO Corporation. The gifts were claimed to be worth more than $250,000. On October 27, 2008, Stevens was convicted on all seven counts.

In February 2009, an FBI agent filed a whistleblower affidavit, alleging that prosecutors and FBI agents conspired to withhold and conceal evidence that could have resulted in Stevens' acquittal. The affidavit alleged that prosecutors intentionally sent a key witness back home to Alaska. The affidavit also alleged that the prosecutors intentionally withheld *Brady* material including both a redacted witness statement and a memorandum that stated that Senator Stevens probably would have paid for the gifts if asked.

Prior to Steven's sentencing date, United States Attorney Eric Holder filed a motion to set aside the verdict and dismiss the indictment. The trial judge signed the order vacating the conviction and dismissing the indictment. The judge also said that it was the worst case of prosecutorial misconduct he had ever seen.

How ironic! The prosecutors who alleged that Senator Stevens was guilty of the crime of failure to disclose failed to disclose *Brady* material.

A 500-page Special Counsel's Report filed on March 15, 2012, stated: "The investigation and prosecution of U.S. Senator Ted Stevens were permeated by the systematic concealment of significant exculpatory evidence which would have independently corroborated Senator Stevens's defense and his testimony, and seriously damaged the testimony and credibility of the government's key witness."

This a situation where prosecutors didn't just commit prosecutor error, and the label of "prosecutorial misconduct" is fitting.

The Senator Ted Stevens case illustrates how severe the consequences of the *Brady* violations can be. Charges were dismissed. The prosecutors were excoriated by the trial judge and the Special Counsel's Report. In addition, during the investigation of prosecutorial misconduct, Nicholas Marsh, a member of the prosecution team, committed suicide probably because of the disgrace.

Material Held by Others

The United States Supreme Court in *Kyles v. Whitley*, 115 S. Ct. 1555 (1995) held that the prosecutor was responsible for learning about exculpatory materials held by members of the prosecution team as follows:

> This in turn means that the individual prosecutor has a duty to learn of any favorable evidence known to others acting on the government's behalf in the case, including the police. . .

CONTACTS WITH JUDGE, WITNESSES AND OTHERS

Communicating with Persons Represented by Counsel

Model Rule of Professional Conduct 4.2 provides:

> In representing a client, a lawyer shall not communicate about the subject of the representation

with a person the lawyer knows to be represented by another lawyer in the matter, unless the lawyer has the consent of the other lawyer or is authorized to do so by law or a court order.

Dealing with an Unrepresented Person

Model Rule of Professional Conduct 4.3 states:

In dealing on behalf of a client with a person who is not represented by counsel, a lawyer shall not state or imply that the lawyer is disinterested. When the lawyer knows or reasonably should know that the unrepresented person misunderstands the lawyer's role in the matter, the lawyer shall make reasonable efforts to correct the misunderstanding. . .

Barricading a Witness

Model Rule of Professional Conduct 3.4(a) provides

A lawyer shall not unlawfully obstruct another party' s access to evidence . . . A lawyer shall not counsel or assist another person to do any such act;

Judicial and Juror Contacts

Model Rule of Professional Conduct 3.5 states that a lawyer shall not:

(a) seek to influence a judge, juror, prospective juror or other official by means prohibited by law;

(b) communicate ex parte with such a person during the proceeding unless authorized to do so by law or court order

Regarding contact with a juror, Model Rule of Professional Conduct 3.5 (c) provides that a lawyer shall not communicate with a juror or prospective juror after discharge of the jury if:

(1) the communication is prohibited by law or court order;

(2) the juror has made known to the lawyer a desire not to communicate; or

(3) the communication involves misrepresentation, coercion, duress or harassment

. . .

Court rules and statutes afford each side a number of peremptory challenges, also referred as a "strikes" in some courts. A party may freely exercise a peremptory challenge against a prospective juror without having to state a reason for the challenge. *Batson v. Kentucky*, 476 U.S. 79 (1986) and related case law bar the improper exercising of a peremptory challenge based on the prospective juror's membership in a cognizable group (race, color, religion, sex, national origin, or economic status). *Batson* held that a state prosecutor could not exercise a peremptory challenge based on race because it violated the Equal Protection Clause rights of both the defendant and the jurors. Later, the United States Supreme Court extended the *Batson* doctrine to civil cases. *Edmonson v. Leesville Concrete Co.*, 500 U.S. 614 (1991); *J.E.B. v. Ala. ex rel. T.B.*, 511 U.S. 127 (1994). Defendants in criminal cases are also subject to *Batson* and may not improperly exercise peremptory challenges. *Georgia v. McCollum*, 505 U.S. 42 (1992).

The prosecutor, as a quasi-judicial officer, is to confine opening statement remarks to statements of fact that the prosecutor expects to prove. Inflammatory oratory is to be avoided. The prosecutor's factual assertions are to be made in good faith and the trial judge has wide discretion in determining whether the prosecutor acted in good faith. 16 A.L.R. 4th 810 Sec. 7(a), (b) (1982).

See the section on closing argument because the statements that a prosecutor is prohibited from making in closing argument likewise constitute error if uttered during opening statement.

INADMISSIBLE VISUALS

The general rule is that if the content of a trial visual is inadmissible, the prosecutor commits error by introducing the visual at trial. It is the content, not the nature of the visual (such as a PowerPoint presentation), that counts. If the content of a visual is inadmissible, displaying it to the jury ordinarily will result in a mistrial or reversal unless the appellate court finds that the error was harmless and was cured by an instruction as it did in *United States v. Burns,* 298 F.3d 523 (6th Cir. 2002)).

PERSONAL OPINION IN THE VISUAL

As has been previously discussed, it is unethical for an attorney to state certain personal opinions during trial. Model Rule of Professional Conduct 3.4 "Fairness to Opposing Party and Counsel" states:

> A lawyer shall not: . . . (e) in trial, . . . state a personal opinion as to the justness of a cause, the credibility of a witness, the culpability of a civil litigant or the guilt or innocence of an accused;

In *In the Matter of Personal Restraint of Edward Michael Glasmann,* 175 Wash.2d 696, 286 P.3d 673 (2012), the Washington Supreme Court condemned the prosecutor's expression of a personal opinion in a closing argument PowerPoint presentation as follows:

> A prosecutor could never shout in closing argument that "Glasmann is guilty, guilty, guilty!" and it would be highly prejudicial to do so. Doing this visually through use of slides showing Glasmann's battered face and superimposing red capital letters (red, the color of blood and the color used to denote losses) is even more prejudicial. *See Gregory,* 158 Wash.2d at 866–67, 147 P.3d 1201.

"[V]isual arguments manipulate audiences by harnessing rapid unconscious or emotional reasoning processes and by exploiting the fact that we do not generally question the rapid conclusions we reach based on visually presented information." Lucille A. Jewel, *Through a Glass Darkly: Using Brain and Visual Rhetoric to Gain a Professional Perspective on Visual Advocacy,* 19 S. Cal. Interdisc. L.J. 237, 289 (2010). Further, [w]ith visual information, people believe what they see and will not step back and critically examine the conclusions they reach, unless they are explicitly motivated to do so. Thus, the alacrity by which we process and make decisions based on visual information conflicts with a bedrock principle of our legal system—that reasoned deliberation is necessary for a fair justice system.

The Washington Supreme Court revisited the issue of the propriety of visuals containing expressions of the prosecutor's personal opinion in *State v. Walker,* 341 P.3d 976 (Wash. 2015). A prosecutor from the same office that prosecuted *Glasmann,* had a PowerPoint presentation of approximately 250 slides with over 100 headed "DEFENDANT WALKER GUILTY OF ASSAULT IN THE FIRST DEGREE." The court's opinion included ten of the computer slides.

DEFENDANT WALKER GUILTY OF PREMEDITATED MURDER (28) Defendant Walker is GUILTY as an ACCOMPLICE to the murder because he SPLURGED ON FRIVOLOUS THINGS	DEFENDANT WALKER GUILTY OF PREMEDITATED MURDER DEFENDANT SPLURGED Defendant Walker purchased 2 safes, a Wii and several games at the Federal Way Walmart
DEFENDANT WALKER GUILTY OF PREMEDITATED MURDER DEFENDANT SPLURGED • Defendant spent $200.00 for dinner at the Red Lobster	

Slides in *State v. Walker* opinion

The Washington State Supreme Court in *State v. Walker, Id.* at 985 held:

> We have no difficulty holding the prosecutor's conduct in this case was improper. Closing argument provides an opportunity to draw the jury's attention to the evidence presented, but it does not give a prosecutor the right to present altered versions of admitted evidence to support the State's theory of the case, to present derogatory depictions of the defendant, or to express personal opinions on the defendant's guilt. *Glasmann,* 175 Wash.2d at 706–07, 712, 286 P.3d 673. Furthermore, RPC 3.4(e) expressly prohibits a lawyer from vouching for any witness's credibility or stating a personal opinion "on the guilt or innocence of an accused." The prosecution committed serious misconduct here in the portions of its PowerPoint presentation discussed above—it included multiple exhibits that were altered with inflammatory captions and superimposed text; it suggested to the jury that Walker should be convicted

because he is a callous and greedy person who spent the robbery proceeds on video games and lobster; it plainly juxtaposed photographs of the victim with photographs of Walker and his family, some altered with racially inflammatory text; and it repeatedly and emphatically expressed a personal opinion on Walker's guilt.

Although a lawyer may not express a personal opinion "as to the justness of a cause, the credibility of a witness, the culpability of a civil litigant or the guilt or innocence of an accused," counsel is not precluded from arguing that the evidence proves the guilt of the accused or that the lack of evidence establishes that the defendant is not guilty. In *State v. Michaels*, the Superior Court of New Jersey Appellate Division reviewed a prosecutor's closing argument involving the use of a puzzle that when it was assembled spelled "guilty" and the court found no error, as follows:

Defendant next contends that the State's display of the word "guilty" on a board during summation was prejudicial misconduct. The prosecutor referred to the jury's task of sorting through nine months of trial evidence as "difficult to assimilate, to collate, to grasp all the elements of evidence in this case as overwhelming as that evidence was." It was "[s]ort of like a puzzle. The pieces of a puzzle." The prosecutors, therefore, illustrated the solution by assembling magnetic letters on the board to spell "guilty," just as the evidence would spell guilty when properly assembled by the jury. Defense counsel objected and stated: "I would appreciate his removing the word guilty because, I think, it implies more than he's entitled to have implied, especially over a prolonged period of time." The court allowed the word to remain on the board.

A prosecutor may comment on the evidence in a vigorous and forceful presentation during summation and draw any reasonable inferences supported by the proofs. ... It is for the jury to accept or reject those inferences and conclusions drawn therefrom. ...It was not improper to use a puzzle analogy to argue that defendant was guilty. There is no basis on which to conclude that placing the word "guilty" on a board had either an immediate impact upon the jurors, or a "subliminal" influence as suggested by defendant. The State was free to contend that the evidence proved defendant guilty as charged. Defendant's contention is clearly without merit. (citations omitted)

ARGUMENT VISUAL

If an argument is improper, displaying the argument in a visual is likewise improper. In *State v. Reineke, 337 P.3d 941* (Or. App. 2014), the Oregon Court of Appeals reversed the defendant's conviction because the prosecutor's PowerPoint presentation infringed upon the defendant's right to remain silent. The presentation argued that the defendant's refusal to speak to the police was a reason he should be convicted of murder. The Oregon Court of Appeals held:

We have no trouble concluding that the jury in this case was likely to draw a prejudicial inference from the prosecutor's references to defendant's invocation in her PowerPoint presentation. The prosecutor's PowerPoint presentation expressly urged the jury to decide that defendant's refusal to speak to the police was one of the four reasons that he was guilty of murdering the victim. The state argues that we should not conclude that defendant was prejudiced because we cannot determine how long the "GUILTY" PowerPoint slides were in front of the jury.

The record, however, demonstrates that the

prosecutor used the PowerPoint presentation in conjunction with her oral argument, which tracked what was on the slides, and that at least three slides implied that defendant was guilty because he "refus[ed] to speak at the police station." Those repeated references to defendant's silence and guilt during closing argument were not subtle, isolated, or fleeting. For the same reason, we reject the state's argument that the prosecutor's oral statements to the jury somehow detracted from the direct implication in the PowerPoint slides that defendant's refusal to speak indicated that he was guilty. We conclude that it is highly likely that the jury drew an adverse inference that defendant's refusal to speak to the detectives was evidence of his guilt.
Id. at 947-48.

In *State v. Milton,* 572 S.W.3d 234, 244 (Tex. Crim. App. 2019), during the sentencing phase of a robbery case, the prosecutor played a YouTube video of a lion trying to eat a human baby through a protective glass, which can be watched in full here— http://www.txcourts.gov/cca/media/

The prosecutor argued that the lion's motive was unchanged and by analogy so was the Appellant's. The Texas Court of Criminal Appeals found that the video presented a "significant potential for unfair prejudice," and concluded as follows:

> Playing a video of a lion trying to eat a baby to argue for a high prison sentence in a simple robbery case was an improper use of a demonstrative aid because the video invited an analogy that was not anchored to the evidence presented at trial. While the State's intended argument was a proper plea for law enforcement, the State by playing the video improperly invited the jury to view appellant's crime and criminal history as more brutal than they were. Consequently, the trial court abused its discretion in allowing the state to play the video. We reverse the

court of appeals and remand the case for harmless analysis.

Id. at 244

MISSTATEMENT OF LAW

A visual that misstates the law can result in a mistrial or a reversal of the verdict. In *California v. Otero*, 210 Cal.App.4th 865, 148 Cal. Rptr.3d 812 (2012). the California Appellate Court described how the prosecutor used a PowerPoint diagram to explain the meaning of the reasonable-doubt burden as follows:

> During argument, the prosecutor told the jury she wanted to give them an example of reasonable doubt. She used a PowerPoint diagram. At the top of the diagram in large bold print were the words "No Reasonable Doubt". The diagram consisted of the outlines of California and Nevada. In southern Nevada was a dollar sign. "Ocean" was printed to the left of California. San Diego was printed inside California, but it was printed in the northern part of the state. Below San Diego was a star and the word Sac. Below that was San Francisco. In Southern California was Los Angeles. The following statement was at the bottom of the diagram: "Even with incomplete and incorrect information, no reasonable doubt that this is California."

> Using the diagram, the prosecutor argued to the jury: "I'm thinking of a state and it's shaped like this. And there's an ocean to the left of it, and I know that there's another state that abuts this state where there's gambling. Okay. And this state that I'm thinking about, right in the center of the state is a city called San Francisco, and in the southern portion of the state is a city called Los Angeles. And I think the capital is Sac-something. And up at the northern part of the state there's a city called San Diego. I'm just trying to figure out what state this might be."

"Is there any doubt in your mind, ladies and gentlemen, that that state is California? Okay. Yes, there's inaccurate information. I know San Diego is not at the northern part of California, and I know Los Angeles isn't at the southern. Okay. But my point to you in this—"
Id. at 869-70 (2012)

Although the court in *Otero* held that the misstatement of law was error, it decided that the error was harmless because the trial judge ordered that it be taken down as soon as the defense objected, and the judge admonished the jurors to disregard it.

The California Appellate Court, in *Otero*, concluded that "(i)t is misconduct for a prosecutor to misstate the law during argument. ... This is particularly so when misstatement attempts "to absolve the prosecution from its prima facie obligation to overcome reasonable doubt on all elements." *Ibid.* Then, the court discussed an "analogous situation" in *People v. Katzenberger,* 178 Cal. App. 4th 1260, 101 Cal. Rptr. 3d 122 (2009) where the prosecutor in closing argument utilized a puzzle of the Statue of Liberty to make a similar argument regarding a reasonable doubt. The court in *Otero* (*Id.* 873) observed:

> In *Katzenberger,* the puzzle was identifiable when six of eight puzzle pieces were in place and "the prosecutor told the jury, 'this picture is beyond a reasonable doubt,' inappropriately suggesting a specific quantitative measure of reasonable doubt, i.e., 75 percent." (*People v. Katzenberger, supra,* 178 Cal.App.4th at p. 1268, 101 Cal.Rptr.3d 122.) The use of a diagram such as the one used in this case is simply not an accurate analogy to a prosecutor's burden to prove beyond a reasonable doubt each and every element of a charged offense.

> Here the diagram was identifiable using but one of eight pieces of information supplied by the diagram

(12.5 percent of the information supplied) and unlike the puzzle in *Katzenberger,* where all pieces contained accurate information, here the diagram contained inaccurate information, making the error more egregious. Not only is the standard of proof reduced to substantially below the condemned percentage in *Katzenberger,* but the jury was informed that reasonable doubt may be reached on such slight proof even when some of the evidence is demonstrably false.

CHAPTER 7. PRESENTATION OF EVIDENCE

PROSECUTOR'S ACTIONS AND STATEMENTS

Besides the important limitation that the prosecutor shall not state personal opinion "as to the justness of a cause, the credibility of a witness, the culpability of a civil litigant or the guilt or innocence of an accused" when addressing the jury, these are the other prohibitions laid out in Model Rule of Professional Conduct 3.4:

> A lawyer shall not:
>
> (a) unlawfully obstruct another party' s access to evidence or unlawfully alter, destroy or conceal a document or other material having potential evidentiary value. A lawyer shall not counsel or assist another person to do any such act;
>
> (b) falsify evidence, counsel or assist a witness to testify falsely, or offer an inducement to a witness that is prohibited by law; . . .
>
> (e) in trial, allude to any matter that the lawyer does not reasonably believe is relevant or that will not be supported by admissible evidence, assert personal knowledge of facts in issue except when testifying as a witness . . .

INADMISSIBLE OR UNCONSTITUTIONAL EVIDENCE

A prosecutor cannot deliberately expose the fact finder to inadmissible or unconstitutional evidence. For example, it is misconduct for a prosecutor to call a witness whom the prosecutor knows will invoke the privilege against self-incrimination—a proper exercise of a constitutional right. *State v. Tanner*, 54 Wn.2d 535, 341 P.2d 869 (1959). Another example is *State v. Mack*, 80 Wn. 2d 19, 490 P.2d 1303 (1971), involving a prosecution for armed robbery where defense counsel on cross-examination asked a defense witness whether he confessed to other robberies to which the witness admitted and on redirect the prosecutor asked who participated in the other robberies with him. The witness answered that the defendant participated with him. The Washington State Supreme Court held:

> A defendant must be tried for the offense charged in the indictment or information. To introduce evidence of an unrelated crime is grossly and erroneously prejudicial, unless the evidence of the unrelated crime is admissible to show motive, intent, the absence of accident or mistake, a common scheme or plan, or identity.
> *Mack*, 80 Wn.2d at 22-24.

The Court went on to reverse even though the trial court had sustained the defense objection and given a curative instruction.

LAWYER AS A WITNESS

A conflict of interests exists when the advocate serves also as a witness. Under Model Rule of Professional Conduct 3.7 (a), "A lawyer shall not act as advocate at a trial in which the lawyer is likely to be a necessary witness..." Exceptions are the situation when the lawyer's testimony "relates to an uncontested issue" or "disqualification of a lawyer would work a substantial hardship on the client."

A lawyer may be an advocate in a trial in which another lawyer in the lawyer's firm is likely to be called as a witness unless precluded from doing so by Model Rules of Professional Conduct 1.7 or Rule 1.9.

WHO'S THE PREVARICATOR HERE? "PITTING IS GENERALLY CONDEMNED"

Cross-examination designed to compel the defense witness to contradict other witnesses by calling them liars has been held to be improper, even classified as "prosecutorial misconduct". It is improper for a prosecutor to cross examine a witness by forcing the witness to pit their testimony against that of another witness, thereby discrediting the other witness. This may be prejudicial and reversible error. *State v. Bryant*, 447 S.E.2d 852 (S.C. 1994) and *Thrift v. State*, 397 S.E.2d 523 (S.C. 1992). *State v. Casteneda-Perez*, 61 Wn. App. 354, 362, 810 P.2d 74 (1991) observed that this practice of pitting is "generally condemned".

North Dakota: In *State v. Foster*, 942 N.W.2d 829, 833-834 (2020), the Supreme Court of North Dakota provided the rationale for barring pitting as follows:

> The task of weighing evidence and assessing credibility is solely within the province of the jury. *State v. Lemons*, 2004 ND 44, 16, 675 N.W.2d 148 (citing *State v. Bell*, 2002 ND 130, 649 N.W.2d 243). Other state courts have recognized it is generally improper to ask one witness to comment on the credibility of another witness or express an opinion regarding whether another witness was telling the truth. See *State v. Morton*, 701 N.W.2d 225, 233 (Minn. 2005) (improper to cross-examine defendant with ''were they lying'' questions where it could lead jury to believe they must think witnesses were lying in order to acquit defendant); *State v. Isom*, 306 Or. 587, 590-92, 761 P.2d 524 (1988) (on cross-examination, prosecutor suggested that contradictory witness was either mistaken or lying); *People v.*

Zambrano, 124 Cal. App. 4th 228, 232, 21 Cal. Rptr.3d 160 (2004) (A prosecutor's "were they lying" questions to the defendant were improper "because they sought defendant's inadmissible lay opinion about the officers' veracity, invaded the province of the jury to determine the credibility question, and were irrelevant to any issue in the case.").

Federal courts have also recognized a prosecutor engages in misconduct by requiring a defendant to call a State's witness a liar. See *United States v. Geston*, 299 F.3d 1130, 1136 (9th Cir. 2002); *United States v. Sanchez*, 176 F.3d 1214, 1219 (9th Cir. 1999). See also *United States v. Sullivan*, 85 F.3d 743, 749 (1st Cir. 1996); *United States v. Boyd*, 54 F.3d 868, 871 (D.C. Cir. 1995) ("It is . . . error for a prosecutor to induce a witness to testify that another witness, and in particular a government agent, has lied on the stand."); *United States v. Richter*, 826 F.2d 206, 208 (2nd Cir. 1987) ("Prosecutorial cross-examination which compels a defendant to state that law enforcement officers lied in their testimony is improper."). We conclude the questioning requiring Foster to give his opinion regarding the credibility of earlier witnesses was improper.

Kansas Collection: The Kansas Supreme Court, in *State v. Manning*, 19 P.3d 84, 100-01, 270 Kan. 674 (2001) listed an array of cases showing how widespread the condemnation of pitting is, as follows:

> Questions, which compel a defendant or witness to comment on the credibility of another witness, are improper. It is the province of the jury to weigh the credibility of the witnesses. See *People v. Riley*, 63 Ill. App. 3d 176, 184-85, 379 N.E. 746, 19 Ill. 874 (1978) (holding that asking the defendant on cross-examination whether the State's witnesses had told a "bunch of lies" was improper);

Commonwealth v. Martinez, 431 Mass. 168, 177, 726 N.E.2d 913 (2000) (noting that it was "improper" to ask the defendant to testify as to the credibility of other witnesses when the prosecutor asked the defendant whether a witness was lying);

Commonwealth v. Ward, 15 Mass. App. 400, 401-02, 446 N.E.2d 89 (1983) (finding that asking a defendant whether a witness lied during his or her testimony is improper and indicating that the error is heightened when a defendant is asked to comment on the testimony of a police officer);

State v. Pilot, 595 N.W.2d 511, 518 (Minn. 1999) (noting that it is the general rule that asking "were they lying" questions of the defendant has no probative value and is improper and argumentative);

State v. Flanagan, 111 N.M. 93, 97, 801 P.2d 675 (1990) (holding that it is "well settled" that asking the defendant whether another witness was lying was improper and is prohibited);

People v. Adams, 539 N.Y.S. 2d 200, 148 A.D.2d 964 (1989) (requiring defendant to characterize police testimony as a "lie" was improper and a tactic to be condemned);

State v. Emmett, 839 P.2d 781, 787 (Utah 1992) (holding that asking the defendant to comment on the truthfulness of another witness's testimony is improper and prejudicial);

Casteneda-Perez, 61 Wn. App. 354, 362, 810 P.2d 74 (1991) (noting that the practice of asking the defendant whether another witness had lied during his or her testimony has been "generally condemned").

This Kansas example of pitting during cross-examination of the defendant comes from part of the transcript quoted in *State v. Manning*:

> Q.   I want to see what you are telling the jury. You are telling the jury that your mom framed you for murder because you wouldn't give her crack at the discount, is that what you are telling us?
>
> A.   I don't know, I don't know why she did it. She probably, everybody knows *she was probably lying*, you never know you never know what crack is or what they are going to say.
>
> Q.   You don't want to call anybody a liar but *your mom is probably lying*?
>
> A. She probably is, I don't know.
>
> Q.   Let me ask you this, was she lying when she said you had a little silver automatic gun?
>
> A.   Yes, I had a big silver shotgun." . . ,

The prosecutor later asked:

> Q. And even though these people, nobody has ever seen them together, none of them claim to know each other, and they tell the story within the day of when it happened, never having been able to get together to talk about it, they all come up with the same story, and *they're all lying, right*? *State v. Manning*, 19 P.3d 84, 101, 270 Kan. 674 (2001)

As was mentioned previously, *State v. Manning*, 19 P.3d 84, 100-01, 270 Kan. 674 (2001) cited this language in *Casteneda-Perez*, 61 Wn. App. 354, 362, 810 P.2d 74 (1991) to explain the reasoning behind the rule:

Unquestionably, to ask a witness to express an opinion about whether or not another witness is lying does invade the province of the jury... A stronger reason for barring such interrogation, however, is that it is misleading and unfair to make it appear that an acquittal requires the conclusion that the police officers are lying. The testimony of a witness can be unconvincing or wholly or partially incorrect for a number of reasons without any deliberate misrepresentation being involved. The testimony of two witnesses can be in some conflict, even though both are endeavoring in good faith to tell the truth.

It is for these reasons that most courts that have addressed the problem, so far as our research discloses, have condemned the practice and will not permit it. Likewise, we find the practice improper and condemn it. It is contrary to the duty of prosecutors, which is to seek convictions based only on probative evidence and sound reason...

While the cross examination of the defendant and other witnesses was improper, the error is not of constitutional magnitude. In such a case, the error is harmless unless there is a substantial likelihood that it influenced the outcome of the trial...

Later in 1995, the Washington Appellate Court, reevaluated its opinion in *Casteneda-Perez* in *State v. Wright*, 888 P.2d 1214, 1223 (Wash. App. Div. 1995) and clarified the situation, as follows:

In sum, we hold that it is generally impermissible to cross-examine a witness in order to elicit an opinion from the witness regarding the credibility of another witness' testimony. Thus, questions of one witness whether another is lying or not telling the truth are improper and constitute misconduct because they are designed to elicit testimony which is both irrelevant and prejudicial. However, where conflicts in the testimony make questions about the discrepancies relevant, questioning a witness about whether he or she believes another is mistaken is permitted. Where no such conflict exists, however, those questions are irrelevant, and objectionable.

Illinois Collection: *People v. Young*, 753 N.E.2d 1046, 1057, 323 Ill. App. 3d 1078 (2001) reversed a first-degree murder conviction in part due to improper cross-examination by pitting, stating:

> In addition to comments, a prosecutor can overstep his or her bounds by conduct as well. As alleged by Young, this can include improper questioning of witnesses. By asking Young to comment on the testimony of the medical examiner, and why other witnesses might lie in their testimony, the prosecutor improperly removed from the province of the jury the duty to determine the credibility of witnesses. While it is certainly a fine line between trial tactics and the using of cross-examination to invade the province of the jury, these facts raise a sufficient specter of impropriety, especially in light of the close nature of the evidence, to question whether Young received the fair trial to which he is constitutionally entitled.

The pitting technique used by the prosecutor prompted Justice Theis to write a concurring opinion directed to just that, as follows:

> In this case, the prosecutor asked defendant several times to comment on the State witnesses' veracity: "So the medical examiner lied when he said that this was an entrance wound?"; "So you can't think of any reason why he (Kenneth Simmons) would lie about what you did, can you?"; "We expect our enemies to lie on us. It (sic) was your friend, wasn't he?"; and "Can you think of any reason why she (Doanita Simmons) would lie?" Defendant answered that he did not know of any reason why they would lie.

The prosecution's practice of asking a criminal defendant to comment on the veracity of other witnesses who have testified against him has consistently and repeatedly been condemned by this court because such questions intrude on the jury's function of determining the credibility of witnesses and serve to demean and ridicule the defendant.
(Here Justice Theis cites twenty-one decisions)

While this practice has generally been deemed harmless error where defendant's guilt was overwhelming, here, as discussed above, the evidence was closely balanced and the credibility of the witnesses was a crucial factor underlying the jury's determination of defendant's guilt or innocence. . .
People v. Young, 753 N.E.2d at 1059-60.

Utah: Utah's Supreme Court explained the dangers of pitting in this way:

The question is improper because it is argumentative and seeks information beyond the witness's competence. The prejudicial effect of such a question lies in the fact that it suggests to the jury that a witness is committing perjury even though there (maybe) other explanations for the inconsistency. In addition, it puts the defendant in the untenable position of commenting on the character and motivations of another witness who may appear sympathetic to the jury.
State v. Emmett, 839 P.2d 781, 787 (Utah 1992) and cited in *State v. Manning*, 19 P.3d 84, 101.

CROSS-EXAMINATION ASSERTION OF FACTS

RPC 3.4 prohibits a lawyer from alluding "to any matter the lawyer does not reasonably believe is relevant or that will not be supported by admissible evidence."

In *State v. Sierra*, 523 S.E.2d 187, 192 (S.C. 1999), the prosecutor cross-examined a defense witness about alleged prior inconsistent statements that the witness made to the prosecutor during a pretrial meeting. The Appellate Court reversed the conviction because no factual basis existed in the record when the question was asked and no extrinsic evidence existed to prove the prior statements.

IMPEACHMENT WITH POST-ARREST SILENCE—*DOYLE V. OHIO*

Doyle v. Ohio, 426 U.S. 610, 49 L. Ed. 2d 91, 96 S. Ct. 2240 (1976) holds that a prosecutor may not comment upon post-arrest silence of a defendant to impeach defendant's testimony at trial. In *Doyle*, when the defendant at trial claimed that he had been framed, the prosecutor sought to impeach the defendant by cross-examining him about failure to tell the story when arrested. *Doyle* held:

> Despite the importance of cross-examination, we have concluded that the *Miranda* decision compels rejection of the State's position. The warnings mandated by that case, as a prophylactic means of safeguarding Fifth Amendment rights . . ., require that a person taken into custody be advised immediately that he has the right to main silent, that anything he says may be used against him, and that he has the right to retained or appointed counsel before submitting to interrogation. Silence in the wake of these warnings may be nothing more than the arrestee's exercise of these *Miranda* rights. Thus, every post-arrest silence is insolubly ambiguous because of what the State is required to advise the person arrested. . . Moreover, while it is true that the *Miranda* warnings contain no express assurance that silence will carry no penalty, such assurance is implicit to any person who receives the warnings. In such circumstances, it would be fundamentally unfair and a deprivation of due process to allow the arrested person's silence to be used to impeach an explanation subsequently offered at trial. . .

(Citations omitted.) *Doyle*, 426 U.S. at 617-19.

People v. Simmons, 689 N.E.2d 418, 422, 293 Ill. App.3d 806 (1998) stated the *Doyle* rule and exceptions as follows:

> Generally, questions and remarks by a prosecutor regarding defendant's post-arrest silence are improper. . . Thus, a defendant's post-arrest silence cannot be used to impeach his testimony or to otherwise create an inference of guilt. . . There are two exceptions to this rule. A defendant's post-arrest silence may be used for impeachment purposes when the defendant testifies at trial that he gave an exculpatory statement to the police when arrested or if the defendant made a prior inconsistent statement to the police after his arrest. . . Although the defendant's post-arrest silence may be used in limited situations for impeachment purposes, it is "not admissible for any purpose in the State's case in chief." (Citations omitted.)

The United States Supreme Court, in *Fletcher v. Weir*, 455 U.S. 603, 607 (1982) held:

> In the absence of the sort of affirmative assurances embodied in the *Miranda* warnings, we do not believe that it violates due process of law for the State to permit cross-examination as to post-arrest silence when a defendant chooses to take the stand.

In *People v. Edwards*, 722 N.E.2d 258263-64, 309 Ill. App. 3d 447 (1999), the State made this argument on appeal that the questioning related to pre-*Miranda* warnings. However, the Appellate Court quoted *People v. Strong*, 215 Ill. App. 3d 484, 488, 574 N.E.2d 1271, 1273, 158 Ill. Dec. 878 (1991) as follows:

> While the decision in *Doyle v. Ohio*, 426 U.S. 610, 49 L.Ed.2d 91, 96 S. Ct. 2240 which held that the State cannot impeach a defendant by his post-arrest silence involved silence after *Miranda* warning, our

courts have consistently applied the ruling to post-arrest silence without reference to the *Miranda* warning.

DANGER ZONE

There is pretty much a consensus that closing argument is a danger zone for prosecutors when it comes to potential for committing error. Comparable to this memorable advice from Atticus Finch in the book *To Kill a Mockingbird*, "Shoot all the blue jays you want, if you can hit them, but remember it's a sin to kill a mockingbird" is this advice in *Berger v. United States* for prosecutors about crafting and delivering a closing argument:

> . . . It is a basic principle of our criminal justice system that prosecutors owe defendants a duty of fairness. . . This duty extends throughout the trial and includes closing statements. Simply put, the prosecutor has an ethical obligation to refrain from presenting improper and prejudicial argument. . . To be sure, a prosecutor is expected to prosecute with earnestness and vigor. . . But, as the United States Supreme Court has recognized, 'while (the prosecutor) may strike hard blows, he (or she) is not at liberty to strike foul ones.' *Berger v. United States*, 295 U.S. 78, 88, 79 L.Ed. 1314, 1321, 55 S.Ct. 629, 633 (1935). . ." *People v. Derr*, 736 N.E.2d 693, 697, 316 Ill. App. 3d 272 (2000). (Citations omitted.)

"One of the most frequent grounds for granting a new trial is that of improper conduct of the prosecutor in closing argument." *State v. Ruff*, 847 P.2d 1258, 1263, 252 Kan. 625 (1993).

CONSIDERABLE LATITUDE

The often-repeated phrase is: "A prosecutor is allowed a great deal of latitude in closing argument." The Pennsylvania Supreme Court expressed it this way in *Com. v. Weiss,* 776 A.2d 958, 968 (Pa.

2001):

> . . . It is also well-settled that a prosecutor must have "reasonable latitude in fairly presenting a case to the jury and must be free to present his or her arguments with logical force and vigor. . . The prosecutor is also permitted to respond to defense arguments.

STANDARD OF REVIEW ON APPEAL

The standard of review on appeal of alleged prosecutor error in closing argument differs depending upon whether or not defense counsel has objected to the prosecutor's argument. For example, the Florida 1st. District Appellate Court in *Hamilton v. State*, 351 So.3d 1275, 1278 (2022), expressed the standards of review as follows:

> To preserve such a claim for appellate review, trial counsel must contemporaneously object to the prosecutor's allegedly improper comments. *Merck*, 975 So. 2d at 1061. Comments to which trial counsel failed to object "are grounds for reversal only if they rise to the level of fundamental error." *Id.* The appellate court "considers the cumulative effect of objected-to and unobjected-to comments when reviewing whether a defendant received a fair trial." *Id.*

EXPRESSION OF PERSONAL OPINION

Now that the general principles for appellate review of alleged prosecutorial error have been covered, this section on the prosecutor's expression of personal opinion leads off the examination of commonly alleged prosecutorial errors during summation.

Model Rule of Professional Conduct 3.3 states:

> A lawyer shall not:(e) . . . state a personal opinion as to the justness of a cause, the credibility of a witness,

the culpability of a civil litigant or the guilt or innocence of an accused;

ABA Standards for Criminal Justice, Prosecution Function and Defense Function, Standard 3-5.8 (3d ed. 1993) says:

> (a) In closing argument to the jury, the prosecutor may argue all reasonable inferences from evidence in the record.   The prosecutor should not intentionally misstate the evidence or mislead the jury as to the inferences it may draw.

> (b) The prosecutor should not express his or her personal belief or opinion as to the truth or falsity of any testimony or evidence or the guilt of the defendant.

Both the prosecutor and the trial judge have a responsibility to ensure that closing argument is kept within proper bounds. "(I)t is fair to say that the average jury, in a greater or less degree, has confidence that (the obligations to produce proper convictions and prevent wrongful ones), which so plainly rest upon the prosecuting attorney, will be faithfully observed. Consequently, improper suggestion, insinuations, and, especially, assertions of personal knowledge are apt to carry much weight against the accused when they should carry none." *Berger v. United States*, 295 U.S. 78, 88, 55 S.Ct. 629, 633, 79 L.Ed. 1314 (1935).

Federal Court: *Stermer v. Warren*, 959 F.3d 704, 725 (2020) referring to the prosecutor's remarks in closing argument held:

> Consequently, insinuations, and especially assertions of personal knowledge are apt to carry much weight against the accused when they should properly carry none." *Berger v. United States*, 295 U.S. 78, 88, 55 S. Ct. 629, 729. L.Ed. 1314 (1935); see also *id.* ([W]hile a prosecutor may strike hard blows, he is not at liberty to strike foul ones.")

Pennsylvania: Prosecutor in closing argument said:

We have heard a lot about the rights of Alvin Joyner, and I'm a lawyer, and I took an oath and I went to law school and I abide by the laws of this land and I love them and I respect them and you, ladies and gentlemen, have borne witness to the unbelievable length our system of justice goes to protect the rights of an accused person.

You have seen how many times I have been stopped during the course of the trial from bringing out things that might have been prejudicial. I have been prevented from telling you a lot of things about this case.

The Pennsylvania Supreme Court found the comments an expression of personal opinion—'For the prosecutor to seek to convey to the jury his own disagreement with the extent of those protections was altogether improper.' *Com. Joyner*, 365 A.2d 233, 1235 (Pa. 1976)

Hawaii: In *State v. Marsh*, 728 P.2d 1301, 1302 (Hawaii 1986), the Supreme Court of Hawaii quoted the prosecutor's closing as follows:

. . . "Ladies and gentlemen, I feel it is very clear and I hope you are convinced, too that the person who committed this crime was none other than Christina Marsh." And later: "I'm sure she committed the crime." Referring to Marsh's testimony, the prosecutor stated: "Use your common sense, ladies and gentlemen. That is not true. It's another lie. It's a lie, ladies and gentlemen, an out-and-out lie." Regarding the alibi witnesses' credibility, the prosecutor said: "You should entirely disregard their testimony because, if you will remember, every one of them lied on the stand . . . I sincerely doubt if she (witness) had seen Christina Marsh there." Of another witness' testimony, the prosecutor stated: "I find that awfully hard to believe."

The Hawaii Supreme Court held:

> Prosecutors are similarly bound to refrain from expressing their personal views as to a defendant's guilt or credibility of witnesses. *United States v. Young*, 470 U.S. 1, 105 S.Ct. 1038, 84 L.Ed.2d 1 (1985); ABA Standards for Criminal Justice, Standard 3-5.8(1980).

> The rationale for the rule is that "(e)xpressions of personal opinion by the prosecutor are a form of unsworn, unchecked testimony and tend to exploit the influence of the prosecutor's office and undermine the objective detachment that should separate a lawyer form the cause being argued." ABA Standards for Criminal Justice, Commentary, at 3.89. The Supreme Court has observed that a prosecuting attorney's "improper suggestions, insinuations, and especially, assertions of personal knowledge are apt to carry much weight against the accused when they should properly carry none." *Berger v. United States*, 295 U.S. 78, 88, 55 S.Ct. 629, 633, 79 L.Ed. 1314 (1935).

The central issue being the credibility of the witnesses, the Court concluded that the prosecutor's "egregious misconduct" of presenting her views on the dispositive issues prejudiced the defendant's right to a fair trial and required reversal.

PERSONAL STORIES

The prosecutor's personal stories venture outside the record and are objectionable. In *People v. Vasquez*, 521 P.3d 1042, 1055 (2022), the Colorado Court of Appeals held:

> At the outset of the prosecutor's closing argument, and over an objection from the defense, a prosecutor told the jurors a brief story about how as a child he was caught secretly lighting matches with a

friend. Defendant argues that the story was irrelevant and impermissibly introduced the prosecutor's "personal s knowledge" into the case. While we agree that the story was improper because it was not confined to the evidence admitted at trial, there is no reasonable probability that it contributed to defendant's conviction.

Illinois: In Illinois, prosecutorial storytelling has run afoul of the personal-opinion prohibition. For example, Illinois reported these three notable cases. First, in *People v. Hayes*, 183 Ill. App. 3d 752, 756, 132 Ill. Dec. 45, 539 N.E.2d 355 (1989), the defendant was charged with aggravated assault and kidnapping for attacking the victim as she walked to a gas station to buy cigarettes. The prosecutor in closing told of her personal experience of being followed by a man when she walked to the store to buy cigarettes. *Hayes* held, "She went far beyond any comment on the evidence and improperly placed the integrity of the State's Attorney's office behind the credibility of this witness." *Hayes*, 183 Ill. App. 3d at 756. The case was reversed because the evidence against the defendant was not overwhelming.

A decade later in Illinois, in *People v. Barraza*, 303 Ill. App. 3d 794, 708 N.E.2d 1256 (1999), again, an aggravated sexual assault case, the prosecutor told a personal story in closing argument to refute the defense attorney's suggestion that the testimony of the two minor victims were not credible because they delayed reporting for two years. The prosecutor's story recounted a conversation with his 10-year-old daughter in which she told him that she would not tell him if she were touched inappropriately despite his instructions to her that she should tell. The Illinois Appellate Court, Second District held:

> The remarks in the present case are similar to those in *Hayes*. The prosecutor attempted to bolster the victims' credibility and elicit sympathy for them by telling a personal story about the conversation with his daughter. These facts were not in evidence and could only serve to improperly bolster the victims' credibility by implying that any child might be reluctant to discuss sexual abuse.

People v. Barraza, 708 N.E.2d at 1259. This conviction also was reversed.

The third appellate decision involving prosecutor storytelling in Illinois is *People v. Shief*, 312 Ill. App. 3d 673, 728 N.E.2d 638 (2000). *Shief* was an armed robbery and aggravated criminal assault case with a mis-identification defense. In rebuttal argument, the prosecutor sought to explain the differences between a witness's ability to describe and ability to recognize using a personal story about how a nurse walked into a hospital room and told the prosecutor that his son would make it, and "At that time, I cannot tell you what she looked like. But I know that I would recognize her in a heartbeat. But today I would tell her she was wrong." Reviewing this story, the Illinois Appellate Court, First District, Third Division held:

> Like the arguments in *Hays* (sic) and *Barraza*, the prosecutor's remarks in this case concerning the situation of his son, albeit somewhat more subtle than the prosecutorial comments in the foregoing cases, were improper because they served only to bolster the credibility of the victim and her testimony. The record is devoid of any facts relating to this experience, and we find the prosecutor's analogy could only operate to have enhanced the victim's credibility by suggesting that all people, particularly Smith, shared the same ability as the prosecutor to identify an individual regardless of the circumstances under which the identification occurred.
>
> The implication before the jury was that Smith was able to easily recognize defendant as her offender because the prosecutor could easily recognize his son's nurse. As presented, the prosecutor's remarks improperly suggested that his ability to recognize a nurse was somehow relevant to the jury's decision regarding Smith's ability to recognize her assailant.
> *Shief*, 728 N.E.2d at 644.

In *People v. Nelson*, 737 N.E.2d 632, 639, 193 Ill. 2d 216 (2000), the prosecutor argued in part: "Whenever a jury acquits a person who has been proven guilty they don't follow their oaths. And if you let the defendant, Tracy Nelson, walk out of this courtroom on this evidence I would suggest you have not lived up to your oaths." Finding the prosecutor's argument in error of such a magnitude that it denied the defendant a fair trial, the Illinois Supreme Court reversed the conviction, holding:

> Indeed, this argument is wholly inappropriate. In *People v. Kidd*, 175 Ill. 2d 1, 50-51, 221 Ill. Dec. 486, 675 N.E.2d 910 (1996), we recognized this type of argument as constituting prosecutorial misconduct. Other courts have come to the same conclusion. Our own appellate court has held that remarks regarding a jury violating its oath by acquitting a defendant are inappropriate. . . The Supreme Court of New Jersey has noted that, "Remarks implying that jurors will violate their oaths if they fail to convict are improper. (Citations) Although the prosecution in a criminal case may use forceful language in summing up the State's case (citation), it may not, as here, explicitly tell the jurors that they are obligated by their oath to return a particular verdict." . . .

ALR on the Subject: *Propriety and Prejudicial Effect of Prosecutor's Argument to Jury Indicating His Belief or Knowledge as to Guilt of Accused – Modern Cases,* 88 ALR3d 449.

VENTURING OUTSIDE THE EVIDENCE

ABA Standards, The Prosecution Function, 5.9 provides:

> It is unprofessional conduct for the prosecutor to refer
> to or argue on the basis of facts outside the record.

National District Attorney Association, National Prosecution

Standards, 85.1 states:

> Closing arguments should be characterized by fairness, accuracy, rationality, and a reliance upon the evidence or reasonable inferences drawn therefrom.

Illinois: This prosecutor's argument went outside the record: "Well, ladies and gentlemen, we can't tell you everything he did after his arrest and he knows it. Maybe when this is over, I will tell you what he did when he was arrested."
People v. Emerson, 455 N.E.2d at 45 (Ill. 1983)

Kansas: Back in 1878, the Kansas Supreme Court, in *State v. Comstock*, 20 Kan. 650, 655 emphatically stated that going outside the records was forbidden:

> Courts ought to confine counsel strictly within the facts of the case; and if counsel persistently go outside the facts of the case in their argument to the jury, then the court should punish them by fine and imprisonment; and if they should obtain verdict by this means, then the court should set such verdicts aside.

Pennsylvania: The Superior Court of Pennsylvania, in *Com. v. Brooks*, 523 A.2d 1169, 1170 (Pa. Super. 1987) stated the rule and rationale this way:

> A prosecutor must limit closing remarks to the facts in evidence and the legitimate inferences that may be drawn therefrom. . . The prosecutor may not argue facts outside the record "unless such facts are matter of common public knowledge based on ordinary human experience or matters of which the court may take judicial notice. . . The reason for this rule is that, because of the very nature of the prosecutor's position, any facts testified to by the district attorney are likely to be accorded great weight by the average jury.

(Citations omitted.)

The prosecutor in closing argued:

> Ladies and gentlemen, last year in Philadelphia (sic) we had 525 homicides

This comment was found to be among other things outside the record and error. *Com. v. Green*, 611 A.2d 1294, 1298 (Pa. Super. 1992)

South Carolina: In *State v. Jones*, 466 S.E.2d 733, 734 (S.C. 1996), the prosecutor referred to the DNA evidence in the O. J. Simpson case and contrasted it with the eyewitness testimony before the jury. The Appellate Court held:

> In making closing arguments, attorneys should stay within the record and its reasonable inferences. . . Therefore, a comparison by the state of this case to a totally unrelated case was improper. However, improper statements must materially prejudice the right of the defendant to obtain a fair and impartial trial. . . We find no prejudice here.
> (Citations omitted.)

In the *Jones'* case, a footnote, the Appellate Court cautioned the bar, "however, that references to any highly publicized case could potentially be prejudicial."

In *State v. Huggins*, 481 S.E.2d 114, 116 (S.C. 1997), a homicide case, the prosecutor cross-examined the defendant about a prior statement supposedly made to her brother about a planned way to kill the victim. The defendant denied making the statement and the statement was never introduced into evidence. During closing, the prosecutor again referred to the statement, and the trial court denied the defense mistrial motion. The conviction was overturned because the improper argument outside the record so infected the trial that it denied the defendant a fair trial.

In *State v. Coleman*, 389 S.E.2d 659, 667 (S.C. 1990), the South Carolina Supreme Court reversed the conviction because the prosecutor argued that he did not call witnesses because they were not involved when there no evidence supporting the prosecutor's assertion.

INFERENCES MAY BE ARGUED, BUT SUGGESTING ADDITIONAL EVIDENCE IS IMPROPER

It is the well-established and generally accepted rule across the country that a prosecutor may neither express nor imply that other evidence existed, which the prosecutor did not introduce at trial.

Illinois: In *People v. Shief*, 728 N.E.2d 638, 312 Ill. App. 3d 673 (2000), the prosecutor made this argument:

> "Let's talk about something because there is something (defense counsel) talked about that we didn't show. Let's talk about police reports. Guess how many police reports you're going to get with you when you go back to that jury room?
>
> . . .
>
> You're not getting any. You know why(?). . .
>
> They're not evidence. You see if I had my way, I would hand you all these police reports and say to you go back in there and say he's guilty(.)"

Reviewing this argument and others, the Illinois Appellate Court, First District, Third Division reversed the conviction and held:

> We also agree with the defendant that the prosecutor's comments about the police reports were equally erroneous. A prosecutor exceeds the bounds of permissible argument where he comments on facts which are inadmissible, or where he suggests that evidence of guilt existed but which, because of its

inadmissibility, cannot be heard by the jury. . . As noted by our supreme court, "an insinuation that leaves the jury to speculate may be more prejudicial than erroneously admitted specific proof."

Contrary to the State's assertion, the prosecutor's statements were not an invited response and went far beyond defense counsel's comments about the reports. The police reports could be used, as the defense did, for impeachment purposes, but could not be used as substantive evidence against defendant. . . The prosecutorial remarks at issue improperly infer that the defense intentionally kept the reports from the jury and that they contained information that would have unequivocally established defendant's guilt and made a trial unnecessary. . .
(Citations omitted.)
People v. Shief, 728 N.E.2d at 644.

In *People v. Emerson*, 455 N.E.2d at 45 (Ill. 1983), this prosecutorial remark was held to be improper as a comment on facts that were inadmissible:

Well, ladies and gentlemen, we can't tell you everything he did after his arrest and he knows it. Maybe when this is over, I will tell you what he did when he was arrested.

California: California offers some remarkable illustrations of prosecutors who ventured beyond the evidence: *People v. Bell*, 49 Cal 3d 502, 538 (1989) (The appellate court found this argument by counsel to be beyond the evidence, factually inaccurate and not a matter of common knowledge: "Those of you who have some medical knowledge know that cocaine is a downer, you get mellow on it. It's not like methedrine which strokes you up and causes you to do irrational acts. Cocaine is a downer. You don't go out and shoot people on cocaine. You make love: you mellow.") and *People v. Sanchez*, 275 Cal. App. 2d 226, 234 (1969) ("While the 9:15

p.m. sale could properly be characterized as 'clandestine,' the prosecutor's comments as to his personal experiences (as a CIA agent) and training were totally irrelevant and beyond the scope of legitimate argument. As stated in *People v. Whitehead*, (1957) 148 Cal. App. 2d 701, 706: 'It is always misconduct for a prosecutor to bring before a jury fact from his own experience which are not to be found in the evidence before them.'').

ALR on the Subject: *Propriety and Prejudicial Effect of Prosecutor's Argument to Jury Indicating That He Has Additional Evidence of Defendant's Guilt Which He Did Not Deem Necessary to Present*, Gregory G. Sarno, 90 ALR3d 646.

PEJORATIVE APPELLATIONS—DENUNCIATORY EPITHETS—NAME CALLING

Name Calling the Defendant

State v. Strickland, 872 S.E. 2d 594, 604 (N.C. App. 2022) explains that while mere name-calling by a prosecutor is improper, the prosecutor is entitled to argue reasonable inferences from the record in summation. The North Carolina Appellate Court held:

> During her closing argument, the prosecution referred to Defendant as ''unpredictable,'' ''impulsive,'' ''angry,'' ''obsessed,'' ''frustrated,'' and ''dangerous.'' All of these statements are reasonable inferences from the record, and a prosecutor may argue all such inferences in closing. See *State v. Alston*, 341 N.C. 198, 239, 461 S.E.2d 687, 709-10 (1995) (''Counsel may, however, argue to the jury the law, the facts in evidence, and all reasonable inferences drawn therefrom.'').

> Furthermore, a prosecutor's remarks that are critical of a defendant, even if derogatory, do not always amount to grossly improper argument. See *State v.*

Larrimore, 340 N.C. 119, 163, 456 S.E.2d 789, 812 (1995) (holding that a prosecutor's characterization of a defendant as "the quintessential evil" and "one of the most dangerous men in the state" did not reach the level of gross impropriety that required the trial court to intervene ex mero motu). Given that the prosecutor's statements are derived from the evidence, are not mere opinions or name-calling, and were not so incendiary as to warrant objection at the time they were made, we hold that the trial court did not err in declining to intervene ex mero motu.

In a footnote, the Appellate Court offered an example of mere name-calling as follows:

The prosecutor's characterization of Defendant based on the evidence differs from improper statements of opinion that amount to nothing more than name-calling. See, e.g, *State v. Jones*, 55 N.C. 117, 133, 558 S.E.2d 97, 107-08 (2002) holding as grossly improper a prosecutor's statements that the defendant was a "quitter, this loser, this worthless piece of .... He's lower than the dirt on a snake's belly." *Id.* at 604

Pennsylvania Collection: *Com. v. Joyner*, 365 A.2d 233, 1235 (Pa. 1976) quoted this language from an earlier decision:

It is no part of the district attorney's duty and it is not his right to stigmatize a defendant. He has a right to argue that the evidence proves the defendant guilty as charged in the indictment, but for the district attorney himself to characterize the defendant as a "cold-blooded killer," is something quite different. No man on trial for murder can be officially characterized as a murderer or as "a cold-blooded killer," until he is adjudged guilty of murder or pleads guilty to that charge.

Joyner held that it was the same thing to call "the present defendant the 'leader of this pack of murderers.'"

A Northwest Sampler: "mad dog," *State v. Music*, 79 Wn.2d 699, 716 (1971); "on the verge of being what I would term an habitual criminal," *State v. Gibson*, 75 Wn.2d 174, 176 (1969); "hoodlum," *State v. Huson*, 73 Wn.2d 660, 662(1968), and again "mad dog," and also "beasts like that," *State v. Perry*, 24 Wn.2d 764, 769 (1946).

South Carolina Collection: South Carolina, a prosecutor's repeated use of the ever-popular epithet "mad dog" resulted in reversal of convictions for burglary, arson and murder. *State v. Hawkins*, 357 S.E.2d 10 (S.C. 1987). In *Hawkins*, the solicitor referred to the defendant by his nickname "Mad Dog" over forty times during the guilt phase and the sentencing. The South Carolina Supreme Court held that it was permissible for the solicitor to make inquiry sufficient to establish identity, but that excessive repetition of "Mad Dog" denied the defendant a fair trial and infected the sentencing proceedings with an arbitrary factor in violation of the Eighth Amendment of the United States Constitution.

However, later, the South Carolina Supreme Court in *State v. Tubbs*, 509 S.E.2d 815 (S.C. 1999) reversed the Appellate Court's reversal of a conviction involving a trial in which the solicitor referred to the defendant by his nickname "Cobra." The Supreme Court noted that the solicitor in *Tubbs* only referred to the defendant by his nickname seven times compared to the forty or more times that the solicitor used the pejorative nickname in the *Hawkins* case, and that in *Tubbs* the first two references to the nickname were not objected to by defense counsel. Therefore, the Supreme Court in *Tubbs* concluded, ". . . We hold that the solicitor's references to "Cobra" during summation, though undesirable, constituted an occasional use of Defendant's nickname and did not infect the entire trial with unfairness as to deprive Defendant due process of law." *Tubbs*, 509 S.E.2d at 818.

California Sampler: California appellate courts have stated that the use of epithets when supported by the evidence were not errors. *People v. Edelbacher*, 47 Cal. 3d 983, 1030 (1989) ("Argument . . . may include opprobrious epithets reasonably warranted by the evidence . . . 'professional robber' . . . 'animal' . . . 'vicious gunman'"); *People v. Duncan*, 53 Cal. 3d 955, 976 (1991) ("Likening a vicious murderer to a wild animal does not invoke racial overtones. Indeed, the circumstances of the murder might have justified even more opprobrious epithets."), and *People v. Rodriguez*, 10 Cal. App. 3d 18, 36 (1970) ("A parasite on the community.")

However, when the evidence did not support the pejorative, the California appellate court disapproved, as it did when the prosecutor "compared defendant's actions to those of Hitler's Brown Shirts, Mussolini's people in Italy and Tojo's in Japan, the Ku Klux Klan . . . ." *People v. Beyea*, 38 Cal. App. 3d 176, 196 (1974).

The Defendant is a "Predator"

How appellate courts have decided cases involving the term "predator" provides some perspective on the issue of whether the application of this term to the defendant is wise.

Kansas and the Northwest: In *State v. Maybin,* 2 P.3d 179, 188 27 Kan. App 189 (2000), the usage of "predator" was denounced on appeal, and Kansas followed the Washington Appellate Court's thinking, as follows:

> The Washington Court of Appeals, however, recently held that referring to a defendant as a predator was prosecutorial misconduct because such tactics were clearly intended to inflame the passion and prejudice of the jury. *State v. Rivers*, 96 Wn. App. 672, 675-76, 981 P.2d 16 (1999) held:

> We agree with the reasoning of the Washington Court of Appeals. For the most part, the use of the word predator is designed to inflame the passion and prejudice of the factfinder. The message the prosecutor often wants to convey by implication, is: Get this predator off the streets, or you or your family might be next.

The Kansas Appellate Court in *Maybin* found the error harmless and not sufficient to require reversal of the conviction.

However, as the Kansas Appellate Court noted in *Maybin*, 981 P.2d at 187-88, this is not the uniformly held view throughout the country on the prosecutor's invocation of the term "predator," citing other jurisdictions holdings, as follows:

> Several other states have refused to find prosecutorial misconduct when the prosecutor refers to the defendant as a predator. See, e.g., *Williams v. State*, 627 So. 2d 994, 996 (Ala. Crim. App. 1992) (referring to the defendant as a predator was a legitimate comment on the evidence); *People v. Hines* 15 Cal. 4th 997, 1062, 64 Cal. Rptr. 2d 594, 938 P.2d 388 (1997) (referring to the defendant as a predator was fair comment on the evidence presented); *People v. Alvarez* 14 Cal. 4th 155, 241-42, 58 Cal. Rptr. 2d 385, 926 P.2d 365 (1996) (calling the defendant a "creep" worse than a "predator" was not prosecutorial misconduct; although it was unnecessarily colorful, the comments were consistent with the evidence;

> *State v. Link*, 916 S.W. 2d 385, 388 (Mo. App. 1996) (calling the defendant a predator was not prosecutorial misconduct; although the court did not condone the use of denunciatory epithets towards defendants, the characterization had no decisive effect on the jury; *People v. Chapin*, 265 A.D. 2d 738, 697 N.Y.S. 2d 713 (1999) (finding no misconduct for referring to the defendant as a predator; although comments were inappropriate, they were not so egregious to warrant reversal in light of the totality of the evidence and the trial court's curative instructions); *People v. Brown*, 252 A.D. 835, 836, 675 N.Y.S. 2d 461 (1998) (calling defendant a predator was not prosecutorial misconduct because any prejudice was ameliorated by the trial court's limiting instructions and the overwhelming proof of guilt); *State v. Trull*, 349 N.C. 428, 454, 509 S.E. 2d 178 (1998) (referring to defendant as a predator was not so grossly improper as to require the

trial court to intervene ex mero motu (voluntarily without objection); *Payne v. Commonwealth*, 257 Va. 216, 226, 509 S.E. 2d 293 (1999) (calling the defendant a predator was fair comment on properly admitted evidence in a sentencing hearing before a jury to determine whether the defendant would receive the death penalty); *Tennant v. State* 786 P.2d 339, 346 (Wyo. 1990) (calling defendant a predator was not prosecutorial misconduct in light of the record as a whole).

Illinois: In *People v. Williams*, 730 N.E.2d 561, 573, 313 Ill. App. 3d 849 (2000), when the assigned error reviewed on appeal was name calling because the prosecutor referred to the defendant as the "king of criminals," the Illinois Appellate Court, Second District observed:

A prosecutor is allowed a great deal of latitude in making closing remarks. . . A prosecutor's improper remarks generally do not constitute reversible error unless they result in substantial prejudice to the accused. . ., such that absent the remarks the verdict would have been different. . . Concerning the parameters of proper argument, the prosecutor may denounce the accused, reflect upon the credibility of the witnesses, and urge the fearless administration of justice if based on the facts in the record and the inferences fairly drawn therefrom. . .

The entire record, particularly the full argument of both sides, must be considered on a case-by-case basis to assess the propriety of prosecutorial comment. . . Where the complained-of remarks are within a prosecutor's rebuttal argument, they will not be held improper if they appear to have been provoked or invited by defense counsel's argument. . . Where a timely objection is made to an improper argument, the trial court can usually correct the error by sustaining the objection or instructing the jury to disregard the remark. . . (Citations omitted.)

When the evidence supported the description of the defendant in disparaging terms, Illinois appellate courts have approved the prosecutor's remark: *People v. Landgham*, 537 N.E.2d 981, 989,182 Ill. App. 3d 148 (1st Dist. 1989) (prosecutor's argument that the defendant was "every mother's nightmare" was found proper when the evidence showed that the defendant beat the ten-year-old boy victim with a table leg over almost his entire body); *People v. Franklin*, 552 N.E. 2d 743, 753, 135 Ill. 2d 78 (1990) (prosecutor's description of the defendant as an "executioner" and "professional hit man" was proper for a witness had testified that the murder was a "hit" during defense counsel's cross) and *People v. Chavez*, 762 N.E.2d 553, 564 (2001) (prosecutor's argument that the defendant was a "smart drug dealer," that he dealt drugs for a living, that drug dealers like the defendant are "hard to get" and "a level up" were according to the appellate court "each constituted a reasonable inference based on the evidence in the record").

On the other hand, in *People v. Williams*, 295 Ill. App. 3d 456, 692 N.E.2d 723 (1998), the prosecutor made value-based arguments, including: "This is a case about good and evil;" "You know from what happened out there on August 28 that we are dealing with evil, wicked, vicious people. . ." Although the Illinois Appellate Court, First District, Second Division found the statements harmless and not warranting reversal, it held:

> In our view, the prosecution flirts with error when its closing arguments depict defendants as being evil persons and victims as good persons. . .

ALR on the Subject: *Negative Characterization or Description of Defendant, by Prosecutor During Summation of Criminal Trial, as Ground for Reversal, New Trial, or Mistrial – Modern Cases,* Thomas M. Fleming, 88 ALR4th 8. Here is a page from the ALR listing just a few of the pejoratives aimed at the defendant.

Defendant is a Prevaricator

State v. Supreme Life, 279 A.3d 448, 454 (2022) explains what a prosecutor may say and should not say about a defendant's prevarication, as follows:

"It is improper for a prosecutor to express his personal opinion on the veracity of any witness." *State v. Rivera,* 437 N.J. Super. 434, 463, 99 A.3d 847 (App. Div. 2014) (citing *State v. Marshall,* 123 N.J. 1, 154, 586 A.2d 85 (1991)). A prosecutor may attempt to persuade the jury that a witness is not credible and in doing so, "may point out discrepancies in a witness's testimony or a witness's interests in presenting a particular version of events." *State v. Johnson*, 287 N.J. Super. 247, 267, 670 A.2d 1100 (App. Div. 1996) (citing *State v. Purnell*, 126 N.J. 518, 538, 60A.2d 175 (1992)).

It is, however, improper for a prosecutor to use derogatory epithets to describe a defendant. *State v. Pennington*, 119 N.J. 547, 576–77, 575 A.2d 816 (1990). "[B]y no stretch of the imagination can it be said that describing defendant as a 'coward,' 'liar,' or 'jackal' is not derogatory. . . . Epithets are especially egregious when . . . the prosecutor pursues a persistent pattern of misconduct throughout the trial." *Wakefield*, 190 N.J. at 466–67, 921A.2d 954 (quoting *Pennington*, 119 N.J. at 577, 575 A.2d 816); see also *State v. Acker*, 265 N.J. Super. 351, 356, 627 A.2d 170 (App. Div. 1993) (" 'A prosecutor is not permitted to cast unjustified aspersions' on defense counsel or the defense." (quoting *State v. Lockett*, 249 N.J. Super. 428, 434, 592 A.2d 617 (App. Div. 1991))).

Pennsylvania: *Com. v. Joyner*, 365 A.2d 233, 1235 (Pa. 1976) stated:

We have held that a prosecutor may not inject "his highly prejudicial personal opinion of appellant's credibility into evidence, thereby clearly and improperly intruding upon the jury's exclusive function of evaluating the credibility of witnesses." (Citation omitted.)

South Carolina: As far back as 1937, the South Carolina Supreme Court in *Major v. Alverson*, 190 S/E. 449, 450 (1937) condemned the argument by an attorney that the defendant in a civil case was a "bare faced liar" and reversed and remanded the case. The Supreme Court held that the argument was not only highly improper argument but also amounted to abuse of the witness. In short, "where counsel applies to a witness or litigant abusive epithets, he will do so at his own peril." More recently, *State v. Blurton*, 537 S.E. 2d 291 (S.C. 2000) held:

> Our supreme court has previously held it is improper to call a party a liar in closing argument. See *Major v. Alverson*, 183 S.C. 123, 190 S.E. 449 (1937). However, not all improper closing arguments require reversal. In criminal cases, "(a) new trial will not be granted unless the prosecutor's comments so infected the trial with unfairness as to make the resulting conviction a denial of due process."

The Court of Appeals went on to hold that this error coupled with others amounted to cumulative error requiring reversal.

Federal: Both *United States v. Moore*, 11 F.3d 475, 482(4th Cir. 1993) (". . . First, while it is true the government's comment were improper and indicative of a shoddy and somewhat paltry closing argument. . .") and *United States v. Cooper*, 827 F.2d 991, 995 (4th Cir. 1987) also condemned calling a defense witness a "liar."

Kansas: *State v. Pabst*, 996 P. 2d 321, 268 Kan. 501 (2000) is the key case in Kansas denouncing prosecutorial statements in closing that the defendant is a "liar." *Pabst* provides not only guidance on what is error but also what is proper argument. *Pabst* held:

> Whether couched in terms of the State or the prosecutor, the asserting that Pabst lied was improper. . . It was also improper for the prosecutor to claim, "We didn't lie to you," in an attempt to bolster the credibility of the State's witnesses. . .

As previously noted, in *State v. Pabst*, 996 P.2d 321, 326, 268 Kan. 501 (2000), the Kansas Supreme Court quoted both Kansas Rule of Professional Conduct 3.4, which is similar to RPC 3.4 (e) quoted earlier, and the applicable ABA Standards to the effect that a lawyer shall not "state a personal opinion as to the justness of a cause, the credibility of a witness, the culpability of a civil litigant or the guilt or innocence of an accused. And the Court went on to hold:

> Pabt's credibility was crucial to the case. The prosecutor placed before the jury unsworn testimony which it should not have considered: his personal opinion on Pabst's credibility and the credibility of the State's evidence. Stating facts not in evidence is clearly improper. . . Accusing Pabst of lying goes far beyond the traditional wide latitude afforded to prosecutors in closing argument. . . Inherent in this wide latitude is the freedom to craft an argument that includes reasonable inferences based on the evidence. When a case develops that turns on which of two conflicting stories it true, it may be reasonable to argue, based on the evidence, that certain testimony is not believable. However, the ultimate conclusion as to any witness' veracity rests solely with the jury.

California: California's appellate courts have reviewed prosecutorial arguments that the inferences from the evidence established that the defendant's testimony and statements were lies and did not contain the prosecutor's personal opinion and found that such arguments were proper. Some of the case law is as follows: *State v. Earp*, 20 Cal. 4th 826, 863 (1999) ("The prosecutor is permitted to urge, in colorful terms, that defense witnesses are not entitled to credence (and) to argue on the basis of inference from the evidence that a defense is fabricated. . .."); *People v. Cummings*, 4 Cal.4th 1233, 1303 (1993) (When supported by the evidence and inferences drawn therefrom, argument that testimony or a defense is 'fabricated' may not, without more, be properly characterized as an attempt to impugn the honesty and integrity of defense counsel."); *People v. Edelbacher*, 47 Cal.3d 983, 1030 (1989), and *People v. Adcox*, 47 Cal.3d 207, 237 (1988) ("Nor was it misconduct for the prosecutor to characterize defendant's version of the events as 'fabrication, and I believe it is a fabrication as the evidence shows it to be, of trying to abandon the crime.' Characterization of the defendant's claim of abandoned intent as 'fabrication' was fair comment on the state of the evidence.").

Pejorative Appellations about Defendant's Attorney

South Carolina: As early as 1924, South Carolina appellate decisions condemned a prosecutor's attacks on defense counsel. In *State v. Atterberry*, 124 S.E. 648, 651 (S.C. 1924) it was held that the prosecutor should not have attacked defense counsel for defending "so plain a case." More recently in *State v. Lunsford*, 456 S.E.2d 918, 922 (S.C. 1995), the South Carolina Appellate Court held:

> We agree, however, the solicitor's comment on the quality of Lundsford's lawyer, to which defense counsel did timely object, was improper. . . Counsel should not express, while arguing to a jury, a personal judgment about opposing counsel, including opposing counsel's standing in the legal community. . . Still, the remark does not warrant a reversal and the grant of a new trial.
> (Citations omitted.)

Illinois Examples: Illinois appellate courts have condemned demeaning comments directed at defense counsel. *People v. Hawkins*, 675 N.E. 2d 642, 645,284 Ill. App. 3d 1011 (1st Dist. 1996) (the conviction was overturned when the prosecutor referred to defense counsel as a "paid advocate.") and *People v. Turner*, 539 N.E.2d 1196, 1204-05,128 Ill. 540 (1989) (although the appellate court did not overturn the conviction on a harmless error finding, it disapproved of the prosecutor arguing, "I have done some defense work before I was a State's Attorney and quite frankly I didn't like to do it because I felt I could never exaggerate enough to be a good defense attorney.").

California Collection: The California appellate courts generally hold that the prosecutor may not attack defense counsel. California provides examples, some notable, of prosecutorial attacks on defense counsel include: *People v. Pitts*, 223 Cal. App.3d 606, 704 (1990) (The prosecutor "vilified the public defender's office several times: '. . . if you throw a brick at a pack of dogs and you hit one of them, he'll holler.' These guys never change. All defense counsel get together and discuss their tactics and do the same thing." Comment found unsupported and improper.) and *People v. O'Farrell*, 161 Cal. App.2d 13, 19 (1958) (Held improper prosecutorial argument: "For a reasonable fee (the defense) will give you a reasonable doubt."

An argument that prosecutors are superior to defense or conversely that defense counsel are inferior is impermissible. *People v. Herring*, 20 Cal. App. 4th 1066, 1073 (1993) (Improper for the prosecutor to argue—believe it or not: "I chose this side and he chose that side. My people are victims. His people are rapists, murderers, robbers, child molesters. He has to tell them what to say. He has to help them plan a defense. He does not want you to hear the truth.").

South Carolina: In closing argument in *State v. McFadden*, 458 S.E.2d 61 (S.C. 1995), the prosecutor commented on defense counsel's objection resulting in evidence being excluded, and the South Carolina Appellate Court commented:

> The supreme court has noted its disapproval of counsel intimating that opposing counsel is trying to conceal something from the jury by objecting to the introduction of evidence. *Cummings v. Tweed*, 195 S.C. 173, 10 S.E.2d 322 (1940)., We do not approve of the solicitor's comment.

The Appellate Court went on to hold that the argument constituted harmless error.

Illinois: *People v. Abadia*, 2001 Ill. App. Lexis 854 (1st Distr. 2001) reversed murder convictions because the prosecutor "lambasted defense counsel" in rebuttal. Defense presented no case and in closing the defense suggested two hypotheses to raise a reasonable doubt, neither of which was supported by evidence. In rebuttal, the prosecutor among other comments argued:

> "The problem is it takes four years for a case like this to go to trial. During the four years, from June 20, 1995, and apparently this morning, it gets four years

for two teams of defense lawyers to come up with and concoct the various theories and ideas of what might have happened and what they wished the evidence would show. . . And the night before closing arguments, apparently they sit around and fantasize and concoct a whole bunch of theories (sic) impossibilities of what could have happened and what may have happened and what probably happened."

. . .

"You should ask yourself why lawyers for these defendants would stand here and make up stories."
People v. Abadia, 2001 Ill. App. Lexis 854 (1st Distr. 2001)

The Illinois Appellate Court, First District, First Division decided that while no evidence supported the defense hypotheses, no evidence contradicted it, and therefore, no evidence established that they were fabricated. This led the Appellate Court to hold:

. . . Unless predicated on evidence that defense counsel behaved unethically, the accusations that defense counsel attempted to create a reasonable doubt by confusion, misrepresentation, deception, and fabrication were irrelevant to the defendants' guilt or innocence, improper and highly prejudicial. . .

After careful review of the record, we cannot characterize the prosecutor's rebuttal argument either as based on the evidence or as invited comment by the defense. (Citations omitted.)
People v. Abadia, 2001 Ill. App. Lexis 854 (1st Distr. 2001)

People v. Abadia, 2001 Ill. App. Lexis 854 (1st Distr. 2001) summed up the governing principles as follows:

While a prosecutor may comment on the persuasiveness of the defense theory of the case as well as any supporting evidence and reasonable inferences drawn therefrom, "it is blatantly improper to suggest that the defense is fabricated, as such accusations serve no purpose other than to prejudice the jury. . . While a prosecutor may comment on defense "counsel's failure to produce evidence promised in opening statement so long as the comments do not reflect upon defendant's failure to testify.". . "accusations of deception and trickery by defense counsel serve no purpose except to prejudice the jury." . . "Comments disparaging the integrity of defense counsel and implying that defense presented was fabricated at the discretion of counsel have consistently been condemned." . .

Our supreme court has held that it is improper for a prosecutor to accuse a defendant's attorney of "lying and attempting to create reasonable doubt by 'confusion, indecision and misrepresentation.'" *People v. Weathers*, 62 Ill. 2d 114, 120, 338 N.E.2d 880, 883 (1975). More recently, our supreme court stated that "*unless based on some evidence*, statements made in closing arguments by the prosecution which suggest that defense counsel fabricated a defense theory, attempted to free his client through trickery or deception, or suborned perjury are improper. (Citations.)'" (Emphasis in original.) *People v. Kirchner*, 194 Ill.2d 502,549, 743 N.E.2d 94, 119, 252 Ill. Dec. 520 (2000), quoting *People v. Jackson*, 182 Ill. 2d 30, 81, 695 N.E.2d 391, 230 Ill. Dec. 901 (1998). "Moreover, 'where a prosecutor's statements in summation are not relevant to the defendant's guilt or innocence and can only serve to inflame the jury, the statements constitute error.' (Citations.)" *People v. Kidd*, 147 Ill. 2d 510, 542, 591 N.E. 431, 446, 169 Ill. Dec. 258 (1992). (Citations omitted.)

It is of no help that defense counsel's argument was

totally improper. The concurring opinion by Justice Cousins in *Abadia* described defense counsel's opening statement as a "bombshell." Defense counsel's statement included assertions that counsel declared the charges false, that the defense assumed the burden of proving the defendant did not commit murder and so on. Then, in closing, defense counsel said in essence that the fact that the defense had not presented a case should be held against defense counsel not the defendant. Justice Cousins wrote, "In my view, this is a case where the arguments by both the state and defense are improper. Unfortunately, when such occurs, justice is thwarted." *People v. Abadia*, 2001 Ill. App. Lexis 854 (1st Distr. 2001)

ALR on the Subject: *Propriety and Effect of Attack on Opposing Counsel During Trial of a Criminal Case*, 99 ALR 2d 508.

Defendant's Own Lawyer Doesn't Believe

Prosecutor: ". . . apparently counsel does not believe his own defendant."

Pennsylvania: *Com. v. Joyner*, 365 A.2d 233, 1235 (Pa. 1976) held that the comment was "completely gratuitous."

Appellate Courts across the nation with some exceptions have held that prosecutors cannot in argument suggest that defense counsel does not believe the defendant is not guilty because it is speculation and prejudicial. *State v. Sloan*, 298 S.E.2d 92, 93 (S.C. 1982) held improper a prosecutor's argument that defense counsel "had not overtly asserted his innocence." And held in part:

> . . . The solicitor's remark invited the jury to speculate concerning the attorney's belief in his client's innocence, and was improper.

California: Likewise, in *State v. Bell*, 49 Cal.3d 502,537 (1989) held:

During his rebuttal argument the prosecutor remarked that defense counsel spent some time on special circumstances issues, "and for a man who says that his client didn't commit the crime, that must be a waste of time. But, on the other hand, he might be worried that he did commit the crime, that must be a waste of time. But, on the other hand he might be worried that he did commit it." It is improper for a prosecutor to argue to the jury as an analysis of the defense argument or strategy that defense counsel believes his client is guilty.

ALR on the Subject: *Propriety and Prejudicial Effect of Prosecutor's Argument Giving Jury Impression That Defense Counsel Believes Accused Guilty*, Gregory G. Sarno, 89 ALR3d 263

Attacking the Defense Theory

As stated in *State v. Liberte*, 521 S.E.2d 744, 746-747 (S.C. 1999):

> Certainly, a prosecutor is entitled to call into question the credibility of a defense. See, e.g., *State v. Lunsford*, 318 S.C. 241, 246, 456 S.E.2d 918, 922 (Ct. App. 1995) ("In telling the jury, 'so don't fall for that,' the solicitor was merely telling the jury that it should not credit defense counsel's argument regarding the absence of fingerprint evidence. A prosecutor may fairly point out 'matters which (the jury) should not consider."), cert. denied (October 20, 1995). Likewise, a prosecutor may "legitimately appeal to the jury to do their full duty." *State v. Caldwell*, 300 S.C. 494, 504, 388 S.E.2d 816, 822 (1990). . . .

Attacking the Smoke-Screen Argument

Illinois: In *People v. Kidd*, 591 N.E.2d at 445 (Ill. 1992), this prosecutorial argument was reviewed:

> I submit to you, ladies and gentlemen, that the defenses raised in this case are similar to a smoke screen.
>
> Just as (defendant) filled this apartment building with smoke on October 28, 1980, the defense in this case is trying to fill this courtroom with smoke today.
>
> Just as though those ten children ran around lost in the smoke on October 28, 1980, in that building the defense in this case is trying to fill this courtroom with smoke today.

Kidd held:

> We believe that the assistant State's Attorney's comments were highly inappropriate and extremely prejudicial for two reasons. First, the assistant State's Attorney did not make just one fleeting inadvertent remark regarding this "smoke screen" metaphor. Rather, he commented *eight times* that defense counsel was "raising a smoke screen," or "filling the courtroom with smoke today," or "hoping that the smoke he raises in this room today will strangle the truth like it strangled the life of the ten children," etc. Thus, this case is unlike other cases in which the prosecutor made only a passing reference to a "smoke screen" theme, and it was held not to be reversible error. . . Second, given that this was an arson case – 10 children perished in fire which defendant is accused of starting – we believe that by repeatedly returning to this "smoke screen" theme and making statements that defense counsel is "hoping that just as those ten children got lost in the smoke," the assistant State's Attorney only inflamed the prejudices of the already emotionally charged jurors.
> *People v. Kidd*, 591 N.E.2d at 447.

Kansas: In *State v. Rodriguez*, 8 P.3d 712, 720, 269 Kan. 633 (2000), the Kansas Supreme Court reviewed the prosecutor's "puff of smoke" argument that went in part as follows:

> When you go to a magic show, a magician comes out and he throws something down on the ground and all of the sudden a big puff of smoke comes up. And all of the sudden something appears that wasn't there before. And the magician has thrown that something down on the ground to make that big puff of smoke to divert your attention.

Regarding this argument, the Kansas Supreme Court observed: "In prior cases, analogies similar to the prosecutor's 'puff of smoke' argument in this case have been found to be within the permissible bounds of rhetoric and not gross or flagrant." However, the "smoke screen" or the "fog, smoke and mirrors" type arguments can exacerbate the situation and be noted by the court in deciding that the defendant was denied a fair trial either when a prosecutor also refers to the defendant and defense counsel as liars (*State v. Lockhart*, 24 Kan. App. 2d 488, 490, 947 P.2d 461, rev. denied 263 Kan. 889 (1997)) or when the prosecutor also attacked defense counsel implying that defense counsel was trying to "fool," "intimidate" and "scare" the jury (*State v. McCray*, 267 Kan. 339, 348-49, 979 P.2d 134 (1999)).

California: California has approved the "smoke screen" type argument provided the argument does not suggest that defense counsel was "obligated or permitted to present the defense dishonestly." *People v. Breau*, 1 Cal. 4th 281, 306 (1991), citing *People v. Bell*, 49 Cal.3d 502, 538 (1989). Other arguments addressing diversionary defenses have been upheld in *California. People v. Visciotti*, 2 Cal. 4th 1, 82n. 45 (1992) ("ink of the octopus" metaphor).

Negative Characterization of Defense Witnesses

Usually, prosecutorial arguments attacking defense witnesses fall within the broad latitude granted counsel in closing. *State v. New*, 526 S.E. 237, 240(S.C. 1999) held:

> . . . . Our Supreme Court has held specifically that "(a) solicitor's argument concerning the credibility of the State's witnesses based on the record and reasonable inferences is not error." *State v. Caldwell*, 300 S.C. 494, 505, 388 S.E.2d 816, 822 (1990), See also *Raffaldt*, supra (the State may comment on the credibility of witnesses in argument). Here, the Solicitor responded to New's objection by indicating her comments were not outside the record, but instead were based on common knowledge: "It's a common known, it's a well-known fact. . . . He has testified against someone, he will be considered—(a rat)." We agree and find the Solicitor's comments regarding Bibb's credibility were reasonable inferences from the evidence in the record. . .

However, a prosecutor cannot go so far as to make arguments concerning witnesses that would deny the defendant a fair trial. A prosecutor's personal opinion about the witness's credibility is not permitted. Illinois appellate decisions have held that it is improper for a prosecutor to state personal opinion about witness credibility. *People v. Davis,* 677 N.E.2d 1340,1348, 287 Ill. App.3d 46 (1997) (prosecutor's remarks that the defense witnesses were the "worst liars he had ever seen testify for a defendant" were improper); *People v. Cole*, 400 N.E.2d 931, 933, 80 Ill. App.3d 1105 (1980) and *People v. Clark*, 448 N.E.2d 926,929, 114 Ill. App.3d 252 (1st Dist. 1983).

ALR on the Subject: *Propriety and Prejudicial Effect of Counsel's Negative Characterization or Description of Witness During Summation of Criminal Trial – Modern Cases*, Thomas M. Fleming, 88 ALR4th 208.

Even the Judge Thinks He's Guilty

With some exceptions, appellate courts generally have held that it is impermissible for a prosecutor to convey to the jury that the judge believes the defendant guilty. For instance, *People v. Thomas*, 558 N.E.2d 656, 663, 200 Ill. App.3d 268 (1990) found that the following argument was improper because it put the integrity of the court behind the prosecution's case: "If the evidence wasn't sufficient in this case, he would have told you it wasn't."

ALR on the Subject: *Propriety and Prejudicial Effect of Prosecutor's Argument Giving Jury Impression That Judge Believes Defendant Guilty*, Gregory G. Sarno, 90 ALR3d 822.

The Effect on the Community—Send a Message

Georgia: *Arnold v. State*, 847 S.E.2d 358, 364 (2020) found no fault in the send-the-message argument:

> It is not improper for a prosecutor to argue that a jury should send a message to the community by convicting a defendant. See *Poellnitz v. State*, 296 Ga. 134, 136 (3), 765 S.E.2d 343 (2014) ("[I]t is not improper for a prosecutor to appeal to the jury to convict for the safety of the community or to argue to the jury the necessity for enforcement of the law and impress on the jury its responsibility in this regard." (citation and punctuation omitted).

Illinois: *People v. Rousey*, 587 N.E.2d at 556, 225 Ill. App.3d 157 (Ill. App. 4th Dist. 1992) held:

> Finally, defendants contend that the prosecutor improperly appealed to the emotions of the juror when he stated that people in the City of Chicago were afraid to travel to and from work because of individuals like defendants, and when he encouraged the jury to "send a message to the community" that violent crime will not be tolerated. The prosecutorial argument in the instant case is similar to the prosecutor's comment in *People v. Harris* (1989),

129 Ill.2d 123, 135 Ill. Dec. 861, 544 N.E.2d 357. In *Harris* the defendant claimed that the following comment was so prejudicial as to deprive defendant of a fair trial:

> Everybody hears about crime. Nobody does anything about it. You have a unique opportunity to actually do something about the crime on your streets. . . You are the only ones that sit between this man, this ticking bomb, and that door. *Harris*, 129 Ill.2d at 159, 135 Ill. Dec. at 876, 544 N.E.2d at 372.

Our supreme court held that the aforementioned remark was "apparently intended to persuade the jurors to convict because by convicting they would prevent both crime in general and further crime by this defendant. As such, (the remarks) were proper. It is entirely proper for the prosecutor to dwell upon the evil results of crime and to urge the fearless administration of the law." *Harris*, 129 Ill.2d at 159, 135 Ill. Dec. at 876, 544 N.E.2d at 372. As in *Harris*, the prosecutor in the instant case told the jurors that they had the opportunity to take action against violent crime. Therefore, the prosecutor's remark in the present case was proper. For the aforementioned reasons, we hold that defendants received a fair trial.

Kansas: Appeals to the jurors as members of the community and argument referring to the effect of the jury's verdict on the community have been held improper. *State v. Gould*, 23 P.3d 801, 809 (2001); *State v. Hays*, 256 Kan. 48, 66-67, 883 P.2d 1093 (1994). A prosecutor argument to the effect that the defendant's conduct should not be tolerated in our community is an appeal to jury sympathy and prejudice and can result in reversal. *State v. Finley*, 998 P.2d 95, 105, 268 Kan. 557 (2000) held:

A prosecutor is under a duty to insure that only competent evidence is submitted to the jury and must guard against anything that could prejudice the minds of the jurors and hinder them from considering only the evidence adduced, such as appeals to sympathy and prejudice. See *State v. Ruff*, 252 Kan. 625, 636, 847 P.2d 1258 (1993). In *Ruff*, we reversed a defendant's conviction because of an improper statement of the prosecutor during closing argument to the effect that the jurors should not allow the defendant's conduct to be tolerated in their county. 252 Kan. At 631, 636. We found that the prosecutor's statement implied that if the jury found Ruff not guilty her conduct would be tolerated, and we further found that the statement was not harmless error. 252 Kan. At 636.

It is worthy of note that one of the arguments frowned upon in *Ruff* was the "send a message" to the community that this will not be tolerated. *Ruff*, 847 P.2d at 1264. *State v. Finley*, 998 P.2d 95, 104, 268 Kan. 557 (2000) went on to catalogue other Kansas cases in which the Kansas Supreme Court held similar prosecutorial arguments improper: *State v. Green*, 254 Kan. 669, 684-85, 867 P.2d 366 (1994) (prosecutor argument that "What you (the jurors) decide will be what our community stands for" was improper but harmless in the absence of a motion for mistrial) and *State v. Zamora*, 247 Kan. 684, 803 P.2d 568 (1990) (reversible error for the prosecutor to argue, "He (Zamora) has raped this victim once. If he is found not guilty, he will get away with it again."). The Kansas Supreme Court, in *Finley* went on to reverse the conviction, holding:

In this case, the remarks of the State were clearly improper. Rather than confining the remarks to the evidence, the prosecutor informed the jurors that they were the ones who enforced the laws in the country

and that "this kind of drug use in our community" could not be tolerated, especially when a person dies, and therefore the jury had to find the defendant guilty.
. .

State v. Finley, 998 P.2d at105.

APPEALS TO PASSION AND PREJUDICE

Appeals to Passions and Prejudice

South Carolina: *State v. New*, 526 S.E. 237, 240 (S.C. 1999), held:

> If a Solicitor's closing argument remains within the record evidence and the reasonable inferences therefrom, no error occurs. . . Undoubtedly, a Solicitor may argue the version of the testimony presented, and furthermore may comment on the weight to be accorded such testimony. . . On the other hand, a closing may be held improper where it appeals to personal bias or arouses the jury's passions or prejudice.
> (Citations omitted.)

Illinois: *People v. Chavez*, 762 N.E.2d 553, 563 (2002) states the rule as follows:

> While prosecutors are afforded wide latitude in closing argument and may argue reasonable inferences from the facts in evidence. . ., "it is improper for the prosecutor to do or say anything in argument the only effect of which will be to inflame the passion or arouse the prejudice of the jury against the defendant, without throwing any light on the question for decision". . .
>
> It is incumbent upon the prosecution under general ethical principles to "refrain from argument which would divert the jury from its duty to decide the case

on the evidence, by injecting issues broader than the guilt or innocence of the accused under the controlling law, or making predictions of the consequences of the jury's verdict.'" *People v. Martin*, 29 Ill. App. 3d 825, 829, 331 N.E. 2d 311. (1975), quoting 1 ABA Standards for Criminal Justice Sec. 3-5.8. (Citations omitted.)

Golden-Rule Argument

Colorado: Arguments to the effect that the jurors should put themselves in the victim's place and consider the victim's suffering and the like have been held to be beyond the bounds of legitimate argument. In *People v. Sanders*, 515 P.2d 167, 177 (2022), the Colorado Court of Appeals stated:

> "Colorado courts have indeed deemed it improper, in the guilt phase of a criminal trial, for a prosecutor to direct the jury to follow the "golden rule" and imagine themselves in the victim's place. *People v. Rodriguez*, 794 P.2d 965, 973 (Colo. 1990). However, prosecutors are afforded considerable latitude when they are replying to arguments made by the defense. *People v. Lovato*, 2014 COA 113, 357 P.3d 212. When determining whether arguments were improper, courts must "weigh the effect of those remarks on the trial, and also take into account defense counsel's 'opening salvo.'

California: *People v. Simington*, 19 Cal. 4th 1374, 1379 (1993) ("Here the prosecutor asked the jurors to place themselves in the position of an innocent victim who is assaulted with a knife and sustains serious injuries. . . We conclude that the remarks constituted an improper appeal to the passion and prejudice of the jury.") and *People v. Pensinger*, 52 Cal.3d 1210, 1250 (1991) (Held improper for a prosecutor to ask the jury to suppose the crime had happened to their children.).

<u>Illinois:</u> *People v. Oliver*, 713 N.E.2d 727, 738, 306 Ill. App. 59 (1999) held:

> Generally, the prosecution should not make reference to the victim's family if it has no bearing on the guilt or innocence of the defendant. . . However, brief and isolated comments often will not amount to reversible error. . . Since the prosecution did not dwell upon the victim's family, the comments were not sufficiently inflammatory to constitute reversible error. . . The comments were brief and incidental and so, in our view, the defendant was not materially prejudiced. . . (Citations omitted.)

Hung Jury is a Time Waster

It is "improper to appeal to the self-interest of jurors or to urge them to view the case from a personal point of view" by making an argument like this: "They need only one vote to block a conviction. If we fail to persuade all 12 of you beyond a reasonable doubt, we persuade 11 of you, it wipes out six months, folks. It's as though it never existed." *People v. Pitts*, 223 Cal. App. 3d 606, 695-96 (1990).

Appeal to Racial Prejudice

<u>Washington:</u> The Supreme Court of Washington reversed a conviction "(b)ecause the race based misconduct (of the prosecutor) was so flagrant and ill intentioned that a timely objection and jury instruction could not have cured resulting prejudice. . ." *State v. Bagby*, 522 P.2d 982, 985 (2023). The Court held:

> The two elements of the constituting reversible error. Were repeated use of the term "nationality" to distinguish the defendant, a Black man who is a United States citizen, from other witnesses, all but one of whom are not Black, and framing of several white witnesses as "Good Samaritans" while conspicuously excluding the sole black witness, who

notably tried to deescalate the first incident at issue. *State v. Bagby, Ibid.*

Citing as legal authority the Washington Supreme Court's earlier decision in *State v. Monday*, 171 Wash.2d 667, 257 P.3d 551 (2011) on prosecutorial misconduct committed by appealing to racial bias, the Court held:

> ...Thus, the defendants are among the people the prosecutor represents, and, as such, prosecutors have a special duty to ensure that the defendant's rights to a fair trial are not violated... A defendant's right to an impartial jury under Article 1, Section 22 of the Washington State Constitution is "gravely violated... when the prosecutor resorts to racist arguments and appeals to racial stereotypes, or racial bias to achieve convictions." —such conviction undermine the integrity of our entire criminal justice system...(citations omitted)
> *State v. Bagby*, supra at 990

<u>South Carolina</u>: Generally, racial epithets employed by a prosecutor in closing argument will result in reversal. In *State v. Hinton*, 43 S.E.2d 360, 361-362 (S.C. 1947), the Supreme Court of South Carolina found the following argument to be without justification and reversed the conviction for this and other reasons:

> I do not ask you to convict the defendants merely because a white man was killed by a Negro. At the last court held here this very month I asked a jury to convict a Negro man who murdered a Negro girl in cold blood, and the jury found him guilty and he was sentenced to the electric chair.

In *Miller v. South Carolina*, 583 F.2d 701 (4th Cir. 1978), the prosecutor's race arguments engendered prejudice so great that automatic reversal was required.

Prosecutor in Tennessee: "And this child embraced the Lord and embraced the word of God and tried to grow. And in the child's growth, he met Don McCary. It is the word of the Lord that this child was learning and that this man was corrupting, and that is what happened to this child."

The Tennessee Court of Criminal Appeals in *State v. McCary*, 119 S.W.3d 226, 254 (2003), disapproved of the argument, stating, "In our view those arguments, replete with inappropriate religious references, were improper" and observed "[w]hether the defendant should be 'damned for eternity' is the exclusive jurisdiction of a far greater authority than the state courts."

ALR on the Subject: *Prosecutor's Appeal in Criminal Case to Racial, National or Religious Prejudice as Grounds for Mistrial, New Trial, Reversal, or Vacation of Sentence - Modern Cases*, 70 ALR4th 664.

Religious and Biblical References

Bennett v. Angelone, 92 F.3d 1336, 1346(4th Cir. 1998) disapproved of a prosecutor's biblical argument, calling it "confusing and unnecessary and inflammatory," but upheld the verdict because it was an invited response to defense counsel's Biblical argument and overwhelming evidence existed.

Generally, appeals to religious prejudice constitute error. In Kansas, it has been held that any effort by the prosecutor reasonably calculated to appeal to invoke religious prejudice is to be condemned. *State v. Smith*, 904 P.2d 999 (Kan. 1995).

ALR on the Subject: *Prosecutor's Appeal in Criminal Case to Racial, National or Religious Prejudice as Grounds for Mistrial, New Trial, Reversal, or Vacation of Sentence - Modern Cases*, Debra Landis, 70 ALR4th 664.

Imputing Threats to the Defendant or Defense Witnesses

South Carolina: In *Mincey v. State*, 444 S.E.2d 510, 511 – 512 (S.C. 1994), the prosecutor argued in essence that the defendant intimidated defense witnesses, and the Appellate Court reversed the convictions, holding:

> . . . References to threats or dangers to witnesses are improper unless evidence is offered connecting the defendant with the threats. . . It would be a "prostitution of justice" to permit evidence that someone attempted to influence a witness by fear or fright without any evidence that connects the defendant with the tampering. . .

> Here the testimony of Scoop Dog and Young was critical to Mincey's claim that he was in no way involved in the drug transaction. The Solicitor's inference that Scoop Dog and Young gave false testimony due to intimidation or threats by Mincey effectively contradicted the defense. There was, in fact, no evidence that Mincey intimidated any of the witnesses. Accordingly, counsel was ineffective in failing to object to the Solicitor's comments and Mincey was prejudiced thereby.
> (Citations omitted.)

Illinois: Illinois has several appellate decisions to the effect that, in the absence of evidence in the trial record, a prosecutor is prohibited from arguing that the defendant intimidated or threatened witnesses to keep them from coming forward because the statement is prejudicial and inflammatory: *People v. Mullen*, 540 N.E.2d 473, 476, 184 Ill. App.3d 539 (1st Dist. 1989) (prosecutor improperly argued that witnesses feared that the defendant would shoot them in the back if they testified when the claim was unsupported by the evidence.); *People v. Armstead*, 748 N.E.2d 691, 703, 322 Ill. App. 3d 1 (1st Distr. 2001) (reversal resulted when the prosecutor argued that the victim was afraid to identify the defendant as the shooter, and the appellate court, citing *Mullen,* held, "Prosecutorial statements that suggest that witnesses were afraid to testify because defendant had threatened or intimidated them, when not based upon the record are highly prejudicial and inflammatory.");

People v. Abadia, 2001 Ill. App. Lexis 854 (1st Distr. 2001), (prosecutor argued that "justice doesn't mean you execute someone and scare off all the witnesses and you get away with it" and this caused the court to also cite *Mullen*, and hold it was reversible error and state, "This outrageous accusation of witness intimidation yet serves to more thoroughly convince us that the prosecution's rebuttal commentary constituted a pattern of conduct designed to inflame and arouse the prejudice of the jury. . ."), and *People v. Johnson*, 559 N.E.2d 1041, 1046, 202 Ill. App.3d 417 (1st Dist. 1990) (the appellate court, besides finding that the following argument referenced inadmissible hearsay, suggested that the defendant intimidated witnesses so they would not testify: ". . . Those people did not want to come into court and testify against Richard Johnson or anybody else. . . They don't want to come in. Just because other people don't want to get involved, does not mean that criminals in this State go free.")

Reducing the Jury's Role and Responsibilities

It is improper to make an argument that lessens the jury's responsibility. For instance, it is error to tell the jury about appellate remedies for defendants in capital cases. *State v. Gilbert*, 258 S.E.2d 890, 894(S.C. 1979).

COMMENTS ON DEFENDANT'S REFUSAL TO TESTIFY

Griffin v. California

United States Supreme Court: *Griffin v. California*, 380 U.S. 609, 610-11 (1965) describes the prosecutor's argument:

> The prosecutor made much of the failure of the petitioner to testify:
>
> The defendant certainly knows whether

> Essie Mae had this beat up appearance at the time he left her bedroom. . . He would know that. He would know how the blood got on the bottom of the concrete steps. . . He would know whether he beat her. . . these things he has not seen fit to take the stand and deny or explain.
>
> And in the whole world, if anybody would know, this defendant would know. Essie Mae is dead, she can't tell you her side of the story. The defendant won't.

The Supreme Court held:

> Comment on the refusal to testify is a remnant of the 'inquisitorial system of criminal justice.' *Murphy v. Waterfront Comm.*, 378 U.S. 52, 55, 84 S. Ct. 1594, 1596, 12 L.Ed.2d 678, which the Fifth Amendment outlaws. It is a penalty imposed by courts for exercising a constitutional privilege. It cuts down on the privilege by making its assertions costly. *Griffin v. California*, 380 U.S. 609, 614 (1965).

Illinois: In *People v. Parchman*, 707 N.E.2d 88, 94, 302 Ill. App. 3d 627 (1999), the Illinois Appellate Court, First District, Fifth Division reviewed the prosecutor's closing, which was in part as follows:

> The Defendant is an armed robber. He is a home invader, and he is a coward. He is a coward. He cannot even get up on that witness stand and look you in the eye and deny that. . .

Citing *Griffin*, the Appellate Court held:

> A criminal defendant has a constitutional right (see *Griffin v. California* . . .) and a statutory right . . . not

to incriminate himself. . . Any comment that is intended to direct the jury's attention to a defendant's failure to avail himself of the right to testify violates the defendant's right to remain silent. . . (Citations omitted.)

Nevertheless, *Parchman* held that the error was harmless given the jury instructions regarding the burden being on the State and that closing is not evidence and the evidence was very strong.

<u>ALR on the Subject</u>: *Violation of Federal Constitutional Rule (Griffin v. California) Prohibiting Adverse Comment By Prosecutor or Court Upon Accused's Failure to Testify, as Constituting Reversible or Harmless Error*, 24 A.L.R. 3d 1093.

Comment on Demeanor of Non-Testifying Defendant

People v. Garcia, 160 Cal. App. 3d 82, 91 (1984) held:

Ordinarily, a defendant's nontestimonial conduct in the courtroom does not fall within the definition of relevant evidence. . . Neither can it be properly considered as evidence of defendant's demeanor since demeanor evidence is only relevant as it bears on the credibility of a witness.

If anything, focusing the jurors' attention on a defendant's courtroom conduct distracts their attention from and may diminish the weight they assign to the permissible factors identified by the instructions as legitimately aiding in the determination whether the defendant committed the alleged offense.

Authorizing the consideration of such demeanor in the determination of guilt or innocence also runs the grave danger of inviting the jury to use character of the accused to prove guilt – something that is wholly improper unless the defendant first presents evidence of good character.

Although the Court of Appeals did not reverse because of the strength of the evidence, the Court did find the comment on defendant's demeanor improper.

The Government's Evidence is Uncontradicted

South Carolina: *State v. Sweet*, 536 S.E.2d 91, 93-94 (2000), which found the solicitor's the-evidence-is-uncontradicted argument improper and not harmless, discussed when the argument is proper and when it is foul, as follows:

> . . . Prosecutorial comment, whether direct or indirect, on the defendant's failure to testify is impermissible. . . Where the solicitor refers to certain evidence as uncontradicted and the defendant is the only person who could contradict that particular evidence, the statement is viewed as a comment on the defendant's failure to testify. . .

> In this case, the assistant solicitor stated only Sweet could rebut Verba and Holliday's testimony. Specifically, he told the jury "nobody else knows what happened that night except Tony Sweet and those two girls," and then stated "there isn't any testimony that conflicts with (the statements of the two girls)." Clearly, the comment referenced Sweet's failure to testify and was not merely a comment on the evidence. . .

> (Citations omitted.)

Illinois: In *People v. Edgecombe*, 739 N.E.2d 914, 319, 317 Ill. App. 3d 615 (2000), the Illinois Appellate Court stated the established rules regarding direct and indirect comment on defendant's failure to testify and the prosecution argument that the State's evidence is uncontradicted, as follows:

> In deciding whether an improper comment has been

made on a defendant's exercise of his right not to testify, the court should consider whether the reference was intended or calculated to direct the attention of the jury to "the defendant's neglect to avail himself of the right to testify." . . In making that determination, a reviewing court must examine the challenged comments in the context of the entire record.

Although the State may comment that the evidence is uncontradicted, even when the defendant is the only person who could have provided contrary proof, there is a line beyond which the State may not go. *People v. Keene*, 169 Ill. 2d 1,21, 660 N.E.2d 901, 214 Ill. Dec. 194 (1995). Specifically, the *Keene* court pointed out that 'the State may not point the finger of blame directly at the defendant for his failure to testify when it was within his power to enlighten the jury. (Citations) Such 'prosecutorial design' crosses the 'danger line' marking the outer boundary of proper commentary." . . . Further explaining the court said, "the State is free to point out what evidence was uncontradicted so long as it expresses no thought about who specifically – meaning the defendant – could have done the contradicting. . . (Citations omitted.)

People v. Edgecombe, 739 N.E.2d at.319.

The Appellate Court went on to find that the prosecutor crossed the line. In *Edgecombe*, only the victim testified to the armed robbery, and rather than stating that the evidence was uncontradicted, the prosecutor repeatedly argued that the victim was the only witness who provided testimony about the armed robbery, that "there's no one that got up there that said anything different," and so on. This led the appellate court to conclude: "These remarks, in our opinion, constituted several impermissible comments upon the defendant's failure to testify or to present any evidence." *People v. Edgecombe*, 739 N.E.2d at 921.

In *People v. Holman*, 469 N.E.2d at 127-28 (Ill. 1984), the following prosecutorial closing argument was reviewed:

> In the Sixth Amendment of the Bill of Rights, there is a small provision which holds and states that the defendant has the absolute right to compulsory process, to process witnesses. He could have produced Anne Williams. All he'd have to do is get a court order from the judge. This judge would order the Sheriff of this County to grab that woman and bring her in a ball and chain and handcuffs, if necessary, and absolutely require her to testify, provided she did not incriminate herself, and there is nothing the State could have done.

Holding that the argument was not error, the Court stated the rules pertaining to the defense-failed-to-call argument, as follows:

> This was represented by the State as a response to defense counsel's earlier suggestion in closing argument that because Williams had been available to the State as a witness but had never been called to testify, it could be inferred that her testimony would have been damaging to the prosecution. Holman's objection was overruled.

> Ordinarily, the prosecution may not comment unfavorably upon a defendant's failure to produce a witness, at least if it is not made clear that the witness was readily accessible to the prosecution with the exercise of ordinary diligence. . . However, reviewing courts in this State have consistently held that comment on the failure of a potential defense witness to testify is permitted when made in response to defense counsel's own reference to the State's failure to call the witness to the stand. . .

In this case, the prosecutor's comments were in response to the defense counsel's argument that "(t)he State says there's an Anne Mae Williams out there somewhere. She's not here. She didn't testify. . . . They didn't bring her here." This statement raised the inference that the prosecutor's case would have been compromised by Williams' appearance. The response was properly limited to the provocation. . ., and although the description of the mechanics of serving a subpoena was perhaps unnecessarily vivid, the prosecutor did not dwell on defense counsel's failure to produce Williams to such an extent as to reflect unduly on Holman's culpability. . .
(Citations omitted.)
People v. Holman, 469 N.E.2d at 128

In *People v. Armstead*, 748 N.E.2d 691, 704, 322 Ill. App.2d 1 (2001), the prosecutor in rebuttal argued:

Counsel did allude to Linda Jamison, Coretha Maclin (phonetic) - - not Matthews, Maclin, and said that, well, they were sitting out there during the shooting. Why aren't they brought in? Well, what she didn't tell you, ladies and gentlemen, is that the defense has the same subpoena power as the State does.

After an overruled objection, the prosecutor continued:

And if they thought for one minute they would have identified anybody else but Sam Armstead as the shooter, they had the opportunity to find those people and you heard no evidence that that happened.

The Illinois Appellate Court, First District, Second Division in *Armstead*, stated the rule regarding the defense-failed-to-call argument:

The burden of proof never shifts to the accused, but remains the responsibility of the prosecution throughout the trial. . . In fact, it is reversible error for the prosecution to attempt to shift the burden of proof to the defense. . . Moreover, a defendant is not bound to produce any witnesses and it is error to comment on his failure to do so. . . However, where the defendant is responsible for injecting a witness into the case or refers to his efforts to secure the witness, it is proper to comment on defendant's failure to produce that witness. (Citations omitted.) *People v. Armstead*, 748 N.E.2d at 704.

Armstead reversed the conviction noting that the defense never injected the names of the witnesses into the case. Rather, the State's witness mentioned two women being present on direct examination. Also, the prosecutor in argument mentioned other names in reference to an alibi and then argued that the defense chose not to call them, and the Appellate court noted that the defendant never mentioned them until the prosecutor injected them on cross. *People v. Armstead*, 748 N.E.2d at 704.

DEFENDANT'S SPOUSE FAILED TO TESTIFY

In *People v. Spenard*, 361 N.E.2d 856, 858 (1977), the Court reviewed a prosecutorial argument asking defense counsel to explain to the jury why the defense did not call the defendant's wife to testify, and held, in part as follows:

> . . . In *People v. Munday* (1917), 280 Ill. 32, 117 N.E. 286, the court stated that the prosecutor may comment upon the failure of the defendant to call a witness only if the witness was available for the defendant to call and not accessible to the State. As stated in a comprehensive opinion in *People v. Mays* (1972), 3 Ill. App.3d 512, 514, 277 N.E.2d 547, 548, however a supplement to the rule developed providing that "potential alibi witnesses interjected into the case by the defendant are deemed unavailable to the prosecution and comment with regard to the

failure of such witnesses to testify is proper. *People v. Gray* (1964), 52 Ill. App.2d 177, 201 NE.2d 756."

The *Blakes* opinion does not discuss the relative accessibility of the alleged alibi witnesses or the question of who interjected their names into the case. Here, defendant clearly interjected his wife's name into the case and thus she is deemed not to be equally accessible to the State although she was present at the trial. Even in the absence of the rule stated in *Mays*, the relationship between the witness and the defendant is material, as demonstrated by the statement in *People v. Carr* (1969), 114 Ill. App.2d 370, 378, 252 N.E.2d 912, 916: "It is a fair inference that defendant's friends and his father were more accessible to him than to the State."

ALR on the Subject: *Propriety and Prejudicial Effect of Prosecutor's Argument Commenting on Failure of Defendant's Spouse to Testify*, Caroll J. Miller, 26 ALR4th 9

RIGHT TO A JURY

In *People v. Herrero*, 756 N.E.2d 234, 245, 324 Ill. App. 3d 876 (2001), the Illinois Appellate Court, First District, Fifth Division reviewed the prosecutor's opening argument as follows: "now they want a jury trial and you have to ask yourselves why do they want a jury trial" and later "These individuals are gamblers, they live on the edge, they hope that they can get one of you to be suckered in, one of you to believe that they are not guilty of possession of a controlled substance with intent to deliver." While the defense objected to the first comment and the objection was sustained, the defense did not object to the second. The Appellate Court found the comment to be misconduct yet affirmed holding the error harmless. The decision states:

> For prosecutor Hughes to have commented on Herrero's decision to exercise his constitutional right

to a jury is outrageous, casting a shadow over the proceedings that simply cannot be ignored. Courts cannot countenance prosecutors invading the substantive rights of the accused by making comments that would penalize a defendant for the use of his constitutional rights. . . (Citations omitted.) *People v. Herrero*, 756 N.E.2d at 245.

MISSTATING THE FACTS

Misstatements of fact in closing argument that constitutes a material factor in conviction can be prosecutorial error and result in reversal. In *People v. Oliver*, 713 N.E.2d 727, 734, 306 Ill. App. 3d 59 (1999), the prosecutor in closing argument stated, "And the other DNA, 1 in 2200, and you can do the math. That's less than five thousandths of one percent. . ." The prosecution on appeal conceded that the math was five one-hundredth of one percent but argued that the incorrect statement was harmless. Although the Appellate Court agreed that it was harmless, the decision's analysis is instructive:

> . . . In *People v. Linscott*, 142 Ill. 2d 22, 566 N.E. 2d 1355, 153 Ill. Dec. 249 (1991), the Illinois Supreme Court reversed an accused murderer's conviction because of misstatements made by the prosecution in closing concerning the physical evidence.

People v. Oliver, 713 N.E.2d at 734 discusses the prosecutor's factual misstatements in *Linscott*, such as: hairs found at the scene had been shown to be the defendant's as opposed to being consistent with the defendant's and the bodily fluids of the nonsecretor defendant were like the recovered nonsecretor fluids despite the evidence that the murder was either a secretor or a nonsecretor. *People v. Oliver*, 713 N.E.2d at 734. *Oliver* then went on to discuss the misstatement under review in that case:

> In the instant case we believe the error was harmless. Prosecutorial misconduct in closing argument merits reversal of a conviction if such misconduct

constitutes a material factor in the conviction. *People v. Linscott*, 142 Ill. 2d at 27, 566 N.E. 2d at 1358. In *Linscott*, the prosecutor several times grossly overstated the hair evidence and the serological evidence. Furthermore, the *Linscott* court noted that the evidence in that case was closely balanced. Unlike the case at bar, there were no eyewitnesses. The only evidence aside from the hair and body fluids was the defendant's dream.

In the case at bar, elsewhere in argument the prosecution correctly said that the figure was 1 in 2,200. The probabilities were only misstated on one occasion. In *People v. Moore*, 171 Ill. 2d 74, 100, 662 N.E.2d 1215, 1226-27, 215 Ill. Dec. 75 (1996), the Illinois Supreme Court held that overstatement of the weight of physical evidence by a prosecutor in closing argument did not deprive defendant of fair trial where the misstatement was isolated and elsewhere the weight of evidence was expressed correctly. Aside from the apparently inadvertent miscalculation of the percentage figure, in our view, the prosecution was quite careful not to overstate the physical evidence . . .
People v. Oliver, 713 N.E.2d at 734-35.

MISSTATEMENT OF A CRITICAL LEGAL PRINCIPLE

In the death penalty phase of *People v. Kuntu*, the majority of the court concluded that the prosecutor erred by arguing that the defendant's lack of criminal history was an aggravating factor and a reason to sentence him to death when it was a mitigating factor. *People v. Kuntu*, 752 N.E.2d 380, 402-03, 196 Ill. 2d 105 (2001) held:

Here, the trial prosecutor argued that the jury should employ the factor in a manner directly opposite to the way in which the legislature intended. Such an argument is clearly improper and prejudicial. The jury was instructed in writing that defendant's lack of prior criminal history is a mitigating factor. However, the jury was also instructed in writing that aggravating factors include any other reason supported by the evidence why defendant should be sentenced to death. The prosecutor argued to the jury that one such reason was the identical factor that the jury was instructed was mitigating, *i.e.*, defendant's lack of a prior criminal history.

Sentencing jurors cannot be expected to engage in a meaningful process if weighing aggravation and mitigation when they are given such irreconcilable directions. Such a misstatement of law in closing argument is improper, particularly where, as here, the legal principle misstated is a critical one in the case. See *People v. Holman*, 103 Ill.2d 133, 170, 82 Ill. Dec. 585, 496 N.E.2d 119 (1984). After reviewing the entire closing argument, we conclude that these improper remarks by the State were so inflammatory that defendant could not have received a fair sentencing hearing or were so flagrant as to threaten deterioration of the judicial process and necessitates the vacator of defendant's death sentence. See *People v. Sims*, 192 Ill.2d 592, 637, 249 Ill. Dec. 610, 736 N.E.2d 1048 (2000).

Reasonable Doubt

People v. Laugharn, 698 N.E. 2d 219, 297 Ill. App. 3d 807 (1998) held:

Generally, attempts by counsel to explain the reasonable doubt standard are disfavored because, "no matter how well-intentioned, the attempt may distort the standard to the prejudice of the defendant". . . However, both the prosecutor and defense counsel are entitled to discuss reasonable doubt and to present his or her view of the evidence and to suggest whether the evidence supports reasonable doubt. *People v. Carroll*, 278 Ill. App. 3d 464, 467, 663 N.E.2d 458, 460-61, 215 Ill. Dec. 447 (1996). In *Carroll*, this court held it was not improper when the prosecutor stated:

> "'Now, we need to prove beyond a reasonable doubt that this Defendant committed the offenses of first-degree murder. It's not beyond all doubt or any doubt, but beyond a reasonable doubt, a doubt that has reason behind it. That's not some mythical, unattainable standard that can't be met. That standard is met ever day in courtrooms.'" *Carroll*, 278 Ill. App. 3d at 466, 663 N.E.2d at 460.

The prosecutor's statements in *Carroll* are almost identical to the prosecutor's statements here. We agree with *Carroll* and hold the prosecutor's statements did not rise to the level of plain error. The statements did not deprive defendant of a fair trial or undermine the entire trial. The average jury understands the concept of reasonable doubt and is not contaminated when it hears the prosecutor say that reasonable doubt has reason behind it, and is an attainable standard, which incidentally, are accurate statements.

In a Kansas case, an argument that suggested that the burden was less than what the jury instruction stated (i.e., defining reasonable doubt as a common-sense burden) has been held improper and the error was considered under the label of "prosecutorial misconduct" in *State v. Mitchell*, 7 P.3d 1135, 1144, 269 Kan. 349 (2000).

In *State v. Gilstrap*, 32 S.E.2d 163, 165 (S.C. 1944), the South Carolina Supreme Court said:

> We have held that where counsel for the defense first injects extraneous argument into the case, the defendant is not in a position ordinarily to complain of the argument in reply. . . But in the orderly administration of justice, it is far more desirable and more in the interest of a fair and impartial trial, for counsel on both sides of a case to keep their arguments within the reasonable limits of the evidence.
> (Citations omitted.)

When defense counsel argued for mercy and compassion, not justice, it was not error for the solicitor to urge the jury not to "cop out" because it was an invited response. *State v. Patterson*, 384 S.E.2d 699, 701(S.C. 1989).

Classic Example—Explaining Why the State Didn't Produce X: *People v. Wilburn*, 263 Ill. App.3d 170, 635 N.E.2d 877 (Ill. App. 1st Dist. 1994) is the classic example of meeting unfair defense argument appropriately. In *Wiburn*, defense counsel in closing argument made an argument that an incident involving the defendant carrying knives never occurred because the prosecution did not call police officers who took the knives away. In rebuttal closing, the prosecutor argued:

> Where are the officers that took her knives away? Where are the officers in the first ten minutes that were there? Counsel has subpoena power same as all the other people in this court. . . . If they were going to help, don't you think they would have been in here.
> . .

The Appellate Court held: "Because the comments were invited, they cannot be relied upon as error on appeal." *People v. Wilburn*,

635 N.E.2d at 888.

AFTERWORD

As the Comment to the Model Rules of Profession Conduct states, the prosecutor is a "minister of justice." The prosecutors whom I have known over the years, with a few exceptions, are dedicated to that role of being a "minister of justice" and to exercising their power for good. They want to do the right thing—to do justice.

And, those right-thinking prosecutors would never commit "prosecutorial misconduct." But, prosecutors, like judges, can commit errors in exercising their power. For example, as we have seen, prosecutors can err when addressing the jury. This *Handbook* is devoted to providing prosecutors with guidance on how to avoid pitfalls as they do their job of seeking justice. The *Handbook* also provides criminal defense counsel with information that will enable them to ensure that their clients get due process.

Made in the USA
Las Vegas, NV
30 October 2023

79994027R00070